HULTON'S PICTURE HISTORIES

GENERAL EDITOR: SIR EDWARD HULTON

The British Theatre

A Picture History of

The
BRITISH THEATRE

by

Raymond Mander and Joe Mitchenson

"The Stage but echoes back the public voice;
The drama's laws, the drama's patrons give,
For we that live to please, must please to live."

*From the Prologue by Samuel Johnson,
spoken by David Garrick on his assuming
the management of the Theatre Royal,
Drury Lane, 1747*

THE MACMILLAN COMPANY
NEW YORK

To
SIR BARRY JACKSON
in gratitude
for
his friendship and encouragement

First Published 1957

Made in Great Britain at the Pitman Press, Bath, England

Contents

Introduction

TO attempt to put between two covers the pageant that is British Theatre and try to convey in pictures the glories of the past is indeed an invidious task. The actor's art is of necessity transitory, and only a small reflection of past triumphs, captured by the artist or photographer, can be fixed for posterity, and when added to by contemporary writing and criticism, these small compensations must be judged in conjunction with the plays and the style of theatre in which they were acted.

Today a new medium has arisen, in the form of the recorded performance. Since the earliest days of the gramophone and its forbears, actors have been persuaded to preserve their voices for posterity. We can still hear Irving, Ellen Terry, Joseph Jefferson, Waller, Tree and Forbes Robertson—to name a few—but only a fleeting reminder of a voice is captured, conveying little of their real art. The recent developments of recording have made it possible for whole performances and plays to be caught in their pristine freshness and saved for future generations. Even this is a doubtful blessing—as so much must depend on the actor's visual art. To us now, listening, the memory of our eyes helps our ears to re-create; but how much will be conveyed without the aid of actual memory only those to come will know.

There is also the Film medium—but this too is treacherous. In the early days, when the cinema was silent, great stage stars were persuaded to make appearances in their famous parts. Often they gave their stage performance, plus heavy mime, which they considered necessary to replace the spoken word; this also can make any critical judgments difficult to assess. With the coming of the "Talkies," naturally the stage actor was in demand; but when one compares, as we still can, a stage and film interpretation of the same part by one actor, it is easy to see that this also will be unfair to a reputation in years to come. Most truly great actors have now mastered both vastly different techniques, but to judge one by the other is unsatisfactory.

We have tried in these pages to show not only the actors themselves but the theatre in which they played, and as much as possible the plays they performed in production.

The story of "Theatre" is not one of a single style of entertainment: from the earliest times, musical pieces, dancing, mime and other forms of diversions have all added to the crazy patchwork that is now designated "Show Business."

We have for the purpose of this book read for "British Theatre"—"British Drama," but not taken "British Drama" to mean a dissertation on the art of the playwright. Therefore we have confined ourselves to the "Legitimate" Theatre, its Tragedies and Comedies, and what, in the course of time, has become part of the classic repertoire.

The family history of the British Musical Theatre, with its aristocratic cousin of foreign blood, Opera, and its less genteel relation the Music Hall, has no place in this volume. We leave its story to be told later.

In choosing the pictures and the plays we have tried to be as representative as possible in each period. We have followed this same method to try to depict theatrical changes in building, setting, production and audience.

At no time in history is a country's Theatre entirely self-reliant. Influences from other countries via the playwright are of course the obvious and most constant means of dissemination of thought and writing. The visits of entire Companies have throughout the ages been a big influence on native contemporary ideas: though often the innovations they have brought with them have proved unpalatable at the time. It was a French company which first brought women to the London stage—to be quickly sent about their business by a shocked middle-class morality. Garrick too had trouble with French players he introduced to London; and though they themselves did not win public favour in the face of British insularity, their visits were reflected in our own theatrical scene. It is not till the beginning of the nineteenth century that we find certain theatres set aside for recognised Seasons of foreign companies and soon visits of great Continental figures like Talma, Mars and Rachel to the major theatres are counted as big events. Their art had far-reaching repercussions on English acting. This pattern of theatrical affairs continued through the nineteenth century. The Comédie Française visited London for the first time in 1879 at the Gaiety Theatre, and the Saxe-Meiningen Company came to Drury Lane in 1881. Sarah Bernhardt after her visits with the Comédie Française, established her own Company and was a frequent visitor to London for the rest of her life. Salvini and Ristori came from Italy; Augustine Daly brought his company from New York and introduced Ada Rehan to London, and as the twentieth century dawned Oto Kawakami and his wife Sada Yacco were in London with a Japanese company; he had made a break with his country's traditional drama and introduced Shakespeare and Ibsen to Japan. The Sicilians, with Giovanni Grasso and their "naked soul" acting shook London in 1908. A German company under Hans Anderson flourished. Regular French Seasons were held at the Royalty Theatre, where Réjane and Jane Hading were seen. Eleanora Duse paid frequent visits to London; in 1895 offering the public an interesting comparison with Bernhardt when they both played *Magda* at the same time.

The War put an end to such exchanges, but the traffic was resumed, though not on such a large scale, after it was over; French, Greek, Japanese, Yiddish, German and Italian Companies fitted into the pattern of theatrical London—and similar visits do so to this day, though pictorially they are not represented in our pages.

We have divided our story into historical divisions; but as we shall see these often do not coincide conveniently with theatrical epochs. Before each division we have given a survey of events and trends of the era, and left the pictures and their captions to convey, we hope, some of the magic of the Theatre.

Before we "Ring up the Curtain" on the First Theatre —a convenient but misleading phrase, since the Elizabethan Theatre had no curtain—let us see what caused the rise of the Drama to sufficient popularity to necessitate the erection of a special building for the purpose of its presentation.

The roots of Drama lie shrouded in the mists of antiquity and religious ritual, though this early history need not concern us here. In the third century the Romans introduced their theatre into Britain. The amphitheatres discovered at Caerleon and Verulamium testify to the existence of the kind of entertainment to which the Romans had been accustomed at home being carried on during their occupation of this country.

After the collapse of the Roman Empire and the descent into the Dark Ages it is not until the tenth century that the Clergy began to introduce organised performances in conjunction with their services. The early Christian Church adopted many of the pagan customs and superstitions which had become part of everyday life, altering them to suit their purposes. The Greek and Roman theatre had consisted of two forms of play—those performed in the Classic theatre, and the performances of the Strolling Players, mostly improvisations, mimes and "playlets." The latter, in the Middle Ages, developed into the Jongleurs and Minstrels, the tradition of which was carried all over Europe. Gradually "The Mummers" appeared, presenting crude plays based on legends, on May Day and traditional Festivals; all this, with Morris Dancing and the like, is a descendant of the pagan rituals incorporated into the Christian Church, and eventually becomes part of the Fair Ground Amusements.

These rural entertainments had remained distinctly earthy and to the Church "profane," and it is in their efforts to do battle with them that they themselves entered the field of the Drama. Simple beginnings were made; priests "acted" a form of Liturgical Drama in the church itself, originally in Latin, it later developed into the vernacular, and it was a distinct part of the services of the Church. Gradually these grew in magnitude and at the Festivals of Christmas and Easter they became elaborate "productions," spreading to all parts of the Church or Cathedral; episodes in the Bible stories told, taking place in different "Mansions" or "Houses" set up in different locations in the building. So vast did this type of "play" grow that the Church itself began to view them with suspicion, as people came for the sake of the "entertainment," not the Church services. The introduction of the vernacular itself had proved dangerous, so the religious authorities tried to stifle that which they themselves had created. This was not easy, as a hold had been gained on the public by this form of "entertainment." The result of the opposition was that it merely left the church building itself and became established in the churchyard, the market square, or on the village green.

By 1300 the "plays" had become completely independent of the Church and had passed into the hands of the local authorities, often the Guilds—presented with amateur performers, sometimes assisted by the bands of strolling players, who continued to act the Mimes and Entertainments at the Fairs. Vast Cycles of Mystery Plays were evolved. The old Church method of presentation was carried on, "Mansions" being set up side by side in a circle in which to carry on the action; as many as 30 or 40 would be used for one Cycle. From this began to develop the travelling form of Mystery Play. Each "Mansion" would be set up on wheels, called a "Pageant," and could be moved from place to place in the town, and the whole Cycle produced as a series of concurrent performances, from street corner to street corner. Descriptions of these "Pageants" have come down to us, they appear to have been on two floors—the upper being the "stage," and the lower curtained round for the use of the performers: "a highe place made like a howse with 2 rowmes, being open on ye tope; (in) the lower rowme they apparrelled and dressed themselves; and in the higher rowme they played."

A step ladder allowed the actors to descend to the street, where it seems the action was sometimes carried on from the upper stage. A stage direction reads: "Here Erode (Herod) ragis in the pagond (pageant) and in the strete also."

That these "Pageants" were grandly decorated is certain, the ornamentation being no doubt of a symbolic character. In one dealing with Adam and Eve we gather that Paradise was full of flowers; and in a Cornish play a direction reads: "Let Paradyce be fynely made, with two fayre trees in y^t and an appell upon the tree and som other frute one the other. . . . a fowntaine and fyne flowers in y^t painted."

The "Pageant" representing "Hell" belched forth flames from the mouth of a Dragon's head, and in the adjoining compartment was seen the torments of the sinful Souls. Accounts for a Coventry performance record that fourpence was paid to a man "for keeping fyer at Hell's mouth." It is probable also that a form of mechanical apparatus was used to make Hell's mouth gape. Sometimes the whole "Pageant" itself was built to represent the subject of the play, for "Noah's Ark" it would represent a ship.

In the Percy Anecdotes is preserved an account for a play acted in 1511 on the Feast of St. Margaret, though unfortunately it is not stated where this took place. The following disbursements were made:—

	£	s.	d.
To Musicians (for which, however, they were expected to perform three nights)		5	6
For players, in bread and ale		3	1
For decorations, dresses, and play books	1	0	0
To John Hobbard, priest, and author of the piece		2	8
For the place in which the representation was held		1	0
To furniture		1	4
For fish and bread			4
For painting three phantoms and devils			6
And for four chickens for the hero			4

The elaborate "Spectacles" were costly to produce, and the expenses were met by a tax on members of the Guild; each individual Guild being responsible for its own "Pageant." A Decree by the York Town Council in 1476 says:—

"that yearly in the time of Lent there shall be called before the mayor for the time being four of the most cunning, discreet, and able players within this city, to search, hear, and examine all the players and plays and pageants throughout all the artificers belonging to Corpus Christi play. And all such as they shall find sufficient in person and cunning, to the honour of the city and worship of the said crafts, for to admit and able; and all other insufficient persons, either in cunning, voice or person, to discharge, ammove and avoid."

The Pageant Master was a responsible and important position. The plays told Old and New Testament stories and Lives of the Saints, and texts of these "Dramas" survive, dating from the fifteenth century. Some are in their entirety, as for Chester, Coventry, York (written between 1350 and 1400) and Wakefield; others have come down to us only in fragments. As the "Cycles" grew, so the "Morality" play emerged. This did not deal with a Biblical subject, but was a dissertation on Man's behaviour—a kind of dramatised sermon or parable on how to obtain salvation, told in allegory. *Everyman* is perhaps the most famous example of this style of play: it dates from about 1495. Many other of these have come down to us.

In both the Mysteries and Moralities gradually humorous elements began to be introduced, and from the Morality it was a short step to the entirely secular Comedy, the first example of which we know is *Fulgens and Lucres*, c. 1497. This is called a "goodly Interlude" and is on a classic subject, for the first time proper names replace abstract titles. Often these plays appear to have been performed by Boy players in the Grammar Schools and specially organised Companies from the Chapels Royal. From 1509 such Companies often appeared at Court and for the public.

The effect of the Renaissance was reaching England from Italy. The re-discovery of the classic plays of Terence, Plautus and Seneca were all to have far-reaching influence, though nearly all this activity was scholarly and amateur. Gradually bands of professional players formed themselves under the protection of noblemen and, strangely, even dignitaries of the Church. The players, officially "retainers" or "Servants," were allowed to play to the public for profit wherever they could find a "platform" on which to act. As the players gained popularity so their number increased; in larger towns the inn yards offered the best opportunities for performance, and landlords would welcome the actors, as bringing good business, the galleried yards provided plenty of space for spectators, often companies would stay in one place for "Seasons." It was now but a short step to the establishment of a permanent home for the players.

Meantime, in the Universities and Inns of Court dramatic acting was encouraged. Various styles of writing emerged: Tragi-Comedies on classical subjects led to the evolution of true Tragedy and true Comedy. The most famous of all early comedies is described as "A Ryght Pithy, Pleasaunt and Merrie Comedie Intytuled *Gammer Gurton's Needle*," written circa 1550. It is followed by *Ralph Roister Doister*, by Nicholas Udall, written circa 1553, probably the first play directly written for public performance in London.

Soon, from the University Dramatists, plays based on the historical Chronicles and other subjects flowed in a long stream. The work of Kyd, Greene and Marlowe leads us directly to the public playhouse. To trace the full history of the drama which emerged in the mid-Elizabethan era and culminated in the work of Shakespeare is not our purpose. We wish merely to give an idea of the dramatic activity all over the country which caused the establishment of the regular theatre.

As the new forms of drama developed and the players gained in popularity, so the Church renewed its long struggle with the stage. New plays were now completely devoid of religious subject-matter, and often the lesser comedies, intended to appeal directly to the "groundlings," had become distinctly ribald in their subject-matter, and probably even more crude and vulgar in their presentation. Now the older religious forms of play which were still performed, were attacked; in 1577 John Northbrook condemned: "Histories out of the scriptures. By the long suffering and permitting of these vain plays, it hath stricken such a blind zeal into the hearts of the people, that they shame not to say, and affirm openly, that plays are as good as sermons, and that they learn as much or more at a play, than they do at God's word preached."

From the Reformation the Church of England was also regarding the old Miracles and Mysteries as Papist propaganda. As early as 1568 performances at York were opposed, and at Chester proceedings were taken against the Mayor for allowing their Cycle to be performed, it was not seen after 1575. Those of York and Wakefield were suppressed in 1576 and 1577.

That this form of Entertainment, though most likely on a smaller scale, was still popular and countenanced by the Church in some districts, is proved by entries in the Churchwarden's accounts at Tewkesbury. For the year 1577 there is an entry:—

> More that is by us pd. unto those whose names are underwritt for the players geare as followeth:

Item to Roberte Collens for payntinge	4s 6d
Item to Roger Mylward for makinge of garmentes	4s 8d
Item to Ric. Westone for makinge a Jerkine	13d
Item for vi sheepe skynns for Christes garmentes	3s
Item to Mr. Fyelde for buckerum for capes	8d
Item for two kippe skines for the thunder heades	6d

(The "kip" was a hide of a young animal. Presumably this last item represents parchment stretched over drums to make "thunder" sound effects.)

In 1583 there is an item of 6d. for "the hyer of the players' beardes," and in 1585 an inventory of church goods includes a list of "players' apparrell":—

> Item 8 gownes and clokes.
> Item 7 Jirkyns.
> Item 4 Capps of greene sylke.
> Item 8 heades of heare for the Apostles and 10 beardes.
> Item a face or vysor for the devyll.

In spite of this occasional activity "Puritanism" was fast on its way, and the struggle between Church and Stage, Court and Civic Authority was to be the main cause of the establishment of the public theatre.

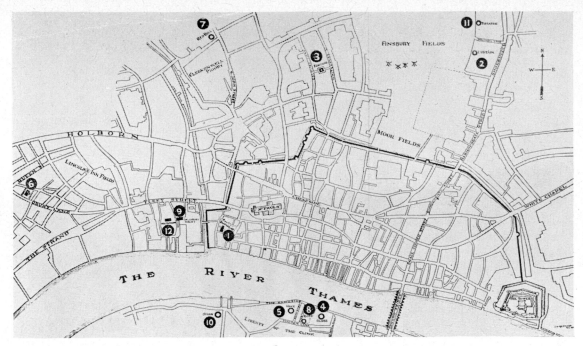

1. Map showing the Theatres of London, built before 1640. From Adam's *Shakespearean Playhouses*, 1917. 1. Black-friars; 2. Curtain; 3. Fortune; 4. Globe; 5. Hope; 6. Phoenix, or Cockpit; 7. Red Bull; 8. Rose; 9. Salisbury Court; 10. Swan; 11. The Theatre; 12. Whitefriars.

PART ONE

Elizabethan & Jacobean

to the Closing of the Theatres
(1576–1642)

For the sake of grouping it is best to include with the Elizabethan period that which immediately followed, until the Puritans closed the theatres during the Commonwealth. As we have seen, playgoing had gained a foothold before the coming of a building designed entirely for the purpose, but from the erection of the first theatre our story really commences.

THE Elizabethan Court was fond of the Players, and so particularly was the Queen, who did what she could to protect the authorised Companies, though the presentation of plays in public was under the authority of the local powers. This became the cause of strife between the class under whose patronage the Drama flourished and the new Puritan influences growing up as represented by the Civic Authorities. The Players claimed it their right to act within the City boundaries, only to be thwarted by various pretexts. In 1572 it was said that gatherings spread the plague; soon a Law was passed ordering Companies to disband, and actors were to be regarded as "rogues, vagabonds and sturdy beggars," unless under noble patronage. In 1575 the Players were expelled from London entirely, though the year before the Queen had granted James Burbage and the Earl of Leicester's men the right to "exhibit all kinds of stage-plays during the Queen's pleasure in any part of England, as well as for the recreation of her own loving subjects as for her own solace and enjoyment."

The Company betook themselves to inn yards outside the City boundaries, and finally in 1576 Burbage built the first permanent public theatre in London in a field near Shoreditch, out of the Lord Mayor's control. He called it simply *The Theatre*. Within a year a rival house opened nearby called The Curtain, taking its name from the locality where it stood, called Curtain Close. Philip Henslow, a shrewd business man, built another opposition playhouse across the River, on Bankside at Southwark, called The Rose in 1588. This district, also out of reach of the City's jurisdiction, was notorious for its Bear Baiting rings and its bawdy houses.

The Swan was built there in 1595. As soon as the theatres opened and favour was shown to the players by the Court, there began to appear tracts denouncing play-going and its patrons. The first appeared as early as 1577, titled: *Treatise against Dicing, Dancing, Plays and Interludes, with other Idle Pastimes*, by John Northbrook. In this he asked, through the mouth of "Youth": "Doe you speake against those places also, whiche are made vppe and builded for such playes and enterludes as the Theatre and Curtaine is, and other such places besides?" To which "Age" replies: "Yea, truly; for I am persuaded that Satan hath not a more speedie way and fitter schoole to work and teach his desire, to bring men and women into his snare of concupiscence and filthie lustes of wicked whoredome, than those places and plays and theatres are; and therefore necessarie that those places and players shoulde be forbidden, and dissolved, and put downe by authoritie, as the brothell houses and stewes are."

Many other denunciations followed. Sermons were preached against the theatre, but the drama gathered strength and became firmly established.

The Companies who acted at these theatres were still titulary under the patronage of noblemen—and their "Servants," calling themselves The Lord Admiral's Men, The Earl of Pembroke's Men, The Lord Chamberlain's Men, and other names; eventually becoming The King's Men, and His Majesty's Servants, which they tradition-ally remained when acting at a Theatre Royal.

Cuthbert Burbage, who had succeeded his father in managing The Theatre, quarrelled with his rivals Henslow and his son-in-law Alleyn, dismantled the building, using the timbers to build a new playhouse on Bankside called the Globe in 1598. This theatre was the scene of the triumphs of the first great English actor Richard Burbage, his brother. Henslow and Alleyn together also built the Fortune Theatre. Alleyn was an actor of great repute, creating the heroes of Marlowe with Henslow's company at their theatres.

These buildings were all open to the sky and, of necessity, Summer theatres, plays being given only in day-light.

In 1597 James Burbage bought part of the old Mon-astery at Blackfriars, including that portion of it which had housed the Boy Players of the Chapels Royal, con-verting it into an indoor theatre. This Children's Com-pany, from 1577 to 1584, was a source of irritation to the professional actors, as they drew away their audiences. To this new indoor theatre Burbage transferred his company during the winter months. As can be seen, the theatre was a thriving concern, though often in trouble with the Authorities and the fast-growing Puritan influence.

The earlier University Dramatists who had provided the plays gave way to the actor-dramatists, of whom Shakespeare is the most important.

This book is not the place to enter into age-old controversy or to give a detailed account of the dramatic writing of each Era that is to be found in the many books which have been written on the subject in all its aspects. Neither is there room or necessity to delve into the specu-lations on methods of play presentation and the details of theatre construction. Many of these are debatable and are still uncertain, and to be dogmatic on any point is to court disaster.

Audiences were strictly divided between the aristo-cratic frequenter of the playhouse and the "groundlings," and the methods of production employed would to us appear naïve—but the audience had to be on the alert and use its imagination.

Costume was at first completely contemporary. Gradually, special details were introduced to signify Country or Class: A "Turkish bonnet" and a scimitar represented an "Eastern" character—no matter what country; a breastplate and a short sword automatically denoted a Roman.

That these extra accoutrements were on a grand scale is borne out by items in Alleyn's inventory, which include—"a scarlet cloak, with two broad gold laces, with gold buttons of the same down the sides, for Lear."—"A purple satin, welted with velvet and silver twist; Romeo's."—"Henry the Eighth's gown."—"Blue damask coat, for the Moor, in Venice."—and "Spangled hose, in *Pericles*."

These methods called for and drew from the drama-tist the necessary word pictures and descriptive passages which make the drama of this era our chief glory and literary heritage. Music was an intrinsic part of the per-formance—flourishes of trumpets and songs all helped to denote and underline the action.

The Companies were, of course, all male. It is difficult for us now to conceive that all Shakespeare heroines were written for Boy actors, who must have attained an astonishing degree of ability to portray such characters.

This, then, was the entertainment of the people, at Court, Masques diverted the nobility. This form of amusement, though not directly connected with the pub-lic stage, was later to have a big influence on it. Inigo Jones, an architect and enthusiast for the theatre, designed many of these Court entertainments, in which often pro-fessional actors took part as well as the nobility. Many were written by Ben Jonson. Jones experimented with movable scenery, as early as 1606, and often designed a special proscenium for each masque. From these be-ginnings were to grow the developments of the Restora-tion stage.

As the theatre began to move indoors and other playhouses were opened, like the Cockpit in Drury Lane

(1616) and Salisbury Court (1629), so the Elizabethan style of presentation gradually changed, drawing on the Court Masques for inspiration. Often the classical masque element was introduced into plays. Indoor audiences became more fashionable, and as a character in Fletcher's *The Woman-Hater* (1607) says:—

> "I'll after dinner to the Stage to see a Play: where when I first enter, you shall have a murmure in the house. Every one that does not know cries 'What nobleman is that?' All the Gallants on the stage rise, vail to me, kiss their hand, offer me their places: then I pick out some one whom I please to grace among the rest, take his seat, use it, throw my cloak over my face and laugh at him: the poor Gentleman imagines himself most highly grac'd, thinks all the Auditors esteem him one of my bosom friends and in right special regard with me."

The middle classes were becoming more and more Puritan and avoided the playhouse as the "Pit of Hell and the Haunt of the Devil." In 1634 William Prynne published a bitter attack on the theatre titled *Histriomastix*. It is strange that in this book, by going into details of the theatre he is denouncing, he should be the means of providing us now with much information which we otherwise would lack. As Prynne had attacked Court Masques as well, and in particular Queen Henrietta Maria for having taken active part, he was immediately seized, fined £5,000, his ears cut off, and put into prison for life, though eventually released under the Commonwealth.

How the theatre would have advanced and where the new reforms were leading can be seen when it is realised that, as early as 1640, Sir William Davenant received from Charles I a patent to erect an entirely new playhouse to give opportunities for the production of plays with rich and elaborate scenery.

The Civil Wars and the rise to power of Parliament and the Puritans stopped all thought of the theatre. The public playhouses were closed and laws passed to prohibit theatre-going. In 1647 it was pronounced that, "all stage-plays and interludes are absolutely forbid, the stages, seats, galleries, etc., to be pulled down; all players, though calling themselves the King's or Queen's servants, if convicted of acting two months before such conviction, to be punished as rogues according to the law: the money received by them to go to the poor of the parish; and every spectator to pay five shillings to the use of the poor."

Other Acts followed, dealing with other forms of amusement. It is interesting to note that, though a legal authority in 1699 stated that he supposed "nobody pretended these things to be Law," no formal repeal has ever taken place. Later Acts referring to the theatre: the Licensing Act of 1737, establishing Censorship and the Monopoly, and the New Licensing Act of 1843 abolishing the Monopoly of the Patent Theatres, did nothing to legalise the social status of the actor. The latter Act simply legalised as many theatres as the Lord Chamberlain chose to license; but any Company playing without such authority or a Magistrate's licence, in the eyes of the Law are still "rogues and vagabonds."

In spite of the laws framed by Cromwell, the Drama was too much a part of the pattern of life to be altogether stamped out at once. Spectators gathered despite the Authorities to watch hastily arranged performances, and Companies who had left London acted in the districts where the Republican control was not so firmly established, keeping the theatre alive. Often Drolls—short playlets made out of portions of longer plays—were presented.

The traditions of English acting were thus kept alive, so that it was possible, when the theatres re-opened officially in 1660, for Companies to be formed which comprised many men who had been Boy actors in 1642.

Also actors like John Lowin were an important link between the two eras. He had first acted in 1602 and worked regularly up to the closing. He was a famous Falstaff, Volpone, and was probably the first Bosola in *The Duchess of Malfi*. He was one of the actors caught giving an illicit performance during the Commonwealth at the Cockpit in 1649, when the raiding soldiers fined the audience on the spot and collected a sum of £3 11s. 4d. Betterton was said to have been coached in the part of Henry VIII by Davenant, on the instructions of Lowin who "had his instruction from Mr. Shakespeare himself," of whom Davenant was said to be an illegitimate son.

Though not strictly part of the story of the Legitimate Theatre, it should be noted that in 1656 Davenant succeeded in obtaining permission to produce an "opera," *The Siege of Rhodes*. This he did at Rutland House, privately, and later at the Cockpit, with the help of John Webb, who had been Inigo Jones' assistant for the Court Masques. This marks the real beginning of the use of scenery for theatrical presentations. During the Commonwealth many of the old theatres disappeared or were put to other uses, so that when the Restoration came a new style of playhouse was able to develop; though carrying on the traditions of the past, it was able to start afresh in the new methods and form a compromise between them.

2. The Globe Theatre, from Hollar's View of London, drawn before 1644 and published 1647. The Globe is on the left. The building on the right is the Bear Baiting house. They were wrongly titled by Hollar.

3. The Interior of the Swan Theatre, from a sketch (now at Utrecht University) by Arend van Buchell, in his Commonplace Book, to illustrate the observations of his friend, Johannes De Witt, who visited the Swan Theatre in 1596. To reconcile certain discrepancies between the diagrammatic sketch and what is known of the Elizabethan Theatre, the suggestion has been put forward that the drawing represents a rehearsal.

4. The Curtain Theatre, from a view of London, circa 1600.

5. The Swan Theatre, from Visscher's view of London, 1616.

6. Model of an Elizabethan Theatre, reconstructed by Dr. Richard Southern for the British Council, 1954.

7. An Elizabethan Stage, from the Frontispiece to Alabaster's *Roxana*, 1630.

8. The Blackfriars Theatre, 1596. A conjectural reconstruction by J. M. Farrar, 1921.

The public theatres of the Elizabethan period were open to the sky and performances took place in daylight. Structurally they were modelled on the Inn Yard, the earlier home of the players. Details of stage construction and the staging method of plays are still debatable. It is certain, though, that as well as the main stage with the audience on three sides of the actors, an inner stage and a balcony were used. Though there was no scenery, movable furniture and properties were introduced. The playwright was obliged in his text to inform the audience if it was night, and the location of his scene. The actors dressed in contemporary, though perhaps more exaggerated, clothes.

The first Blackfriars Theatre—the only playhouse within the City limits—was an indoor one, originally used by the child players from the Chapels Royal. In 1596 James Burbage took over and rebuilt it as a theatre for his Company during the winter months. It remained in use until the closing of the theatres.

9. *Arden of Feversham*. A woodcut in the First Edition, 1592. This anonymous play (c. 1590) was founded on a celebrated crime of the period.

The earliest Elizabethan playwrights, like Greene, Marlowe and Kyd, came mainly from the Universities; to be succeeded by the actor-dramatist. Many of Shakespeare's plays are based on the work of his predecessors.

The early editions of some plays contain crude woodcuts, some of which can be definitely held to represent plays as staged; of these, Nos. 10, 11 and 12 are interesting examples. The cut of Kyd's *Spanish Tragedy* shows an arbour in use, as required by the text. As all women's parts were then played by the boy actors, these too must be represented. It is thought that Nathan Field is seen as Bellimperia in this picture.

The cut of *Arden of Feversham*, the first domestic play founded on fact, may only represent the real crime, and not as it was staged. At one time it was thought that the play was by Shakespeare but this is now rejected.

10. *Friar Bacon and Friar Bungay*, by Robert Greene (c. 1589). A title page woodcut, 1655.

11. *The Spanish Tragedy*, by Thomas Kyd (c. 1589). A title page woodcut, 1633.

12. *Swetnam, the Woman-Hater*, an anonymous comedy. Acted at the Red Bull Theatre, 1620.

13. Robert Greene, playwright (1558–1592).

14. Robert Armin, comedian (fl. 1590–1610).

Little is known of the actors of the period. Some names are recorded in the First Folio of Shakespeare as having acted in his plays. Among these, Lowin played Falstaff, and Armin, Dogberry, in *Much Ado About Nothing*. He was a pupil of Richard Tarlton, the most famous Elizabethan Clown, the "Yorick" of Hamlet. As most of his work was probably extempore, Shakespeare may have had him in mind in Hamlet's advice to the Players. Shakespeare had attempted to confine his actors to the parts written for them and abolish gagging. His first plays date from the early 1590's, towards the end of the Elizabethan era, closely followed by those of Beaumont and Fletcher, Ben Jonson and Dekker, all of whom influenced each other and between them developed the recognisable styles of Drama. Massinger, a close follower of Jonson, is best remembered for his *A New Way to Pay Old Debts*, and Dekker for *The Shoemaker's Holiday*.

15. Richard Tarlton, comedian (d. 1588).

16. Francis Beaumont, playwright (1584–1616).

17. John Fletcher, playwright (1579–1625).

18. Philip Massinger, playwright (1593–1640).

19. Edward Alleyn (1566–1626). First recorded as an actor of repute in 1583. He created *Tamburlaine*, *Faustus* and *The Jew of Malta* in Marlowe's plays. He married the step-daughter of Philip Henslowe.

Alleyn built the Fortune in 1600 with Henslowe, and later became owner of all his father-in-law's ventures. He ceased acting about 1603, and founded the College of God's Gift at Dulwich in 1619.

Sly was with Alleyn's Company and later with Burbage. He is named in the First Folio.

Field, originally a child actor at Blackfriars, graduated to women's parts with Henslowe, and to male leads with Burbage, whom he succeeded.

Richard Burbage, son of James, was the first great English actor, creating Hamlet, Lear, Othello and Richard III, at the Globe, of which his brother Cuthbert was the manager.

Mr. WILLIAM SHAKESPEARES COMEDIES, HISTORIES, & TRAGEDIES.

Published according to the True Originall Copies.

LONDON
Printed by Isaac Iaggard, and Ed. Blount. 1623.

20. Title Page to the First Collected Edition of Shakespeare's Plays, 1623. The engraving of William Shakespeare (1564–1616) by Martin Droeshout, though the subject of much controversy, is one of the few more or less contemporary portraits whose authenticity is beyond doubt.

21. William Sly, actor (d. 1608).

22. Nathan Field, actor (1587–1633).

23. Richard Burbage, actor (1567?–1619).

24. Thomas Dekker, playwright (1570–1641).

25. Christopher Marlowe, playwright (1564–1593). Reputed portrait.

26. John Lowin, actor (1576–1658?).

27. Ben Jonson, playwright (1573?– 1637).

28. Frontispiece to *The Wits*, by Francis Kirkman, a Book of Drolls first published in 1662.

W. J. Lawrence, in his unpublished notebooks, puts forward the conjecture that it may represent the Theatre Royal, Vere Street, where *The French Dancing-Master* had been revived the same year. Most of the other characters depicted: Clause (Beaumont and Fletcher's *The Beggars Bush*), Falstaff and the Hostess (*Henry IV*), Changeling (Rowley and Middleton's *The Changeling*), had recently been revived.

The other actor is Robert Cox as *Simpleton, the Smith*, in a Droll which he played at the Red Bull Theatre, where surreptitious performances were given under the Commonwealth.

PART TWO

Restoration

to the Death of Queen Anne
(1660–1714)

AS previously, it is convenient to include in this period the years up to the beginning of the Georgian era; for though precise lines of demarcation only occur with historical changes, the feeling of an era does sometimes roughly coincide with changes in a dynasty.

After the years of closure the playhouses were quick to begin performances again. Immediately upon the arrival of General Monk in London and the issue of the Invitation to the exiled King Charles to return, Companies sprang into life and performances were given at the Cockpit and at Salisbury Court; but events moved quickly and by July 1660 definite projects were begun to re-establish the theatre on new lines. Firstly, warrants were issued to prepare for grants of Monopoly in theatrical affairs to Thomas Killegrew and Sir William Davenant. These Patents were finally issued in August. Trouble arose owing to the claim of Sir Henry Herbert to the old office of Master of the Revels—an appointment of little glory owing to the two Patentees' rights. Of the ensuing struggle little need be said; it eventually resolved itself to the satisfaction of all concerned.

Let us for a moment, before considering the events which follow, see who the two men were who had gained the monopoly of theatrical affairs. Firstly Sir William Davenant (or D'Avenant)—reputed to be the illegitimate son of Shakespeare, who certainly was his godfather—had made a name for himself as a writer and producer of Court Masques under Charles I. He was created Poet Laureate in 1638. Under the Commonwealth he had managed to evade the ban on playacting, under the pretext that it was "Music and Instruction," receiving permission to produce the *Siege of Rhodes* privately in 1656, followed by his other "Operas": *The Spaniards in Peru* (1658) and *Sir Francis Drake* (1659). By making this "propaganda" against the Spaniards, whom Cromwell hated, he had managed to gain official approval. At the Restoration, on the strength of his previous grant from Charles I in 1640, he was given a Patent to share the Monopoly with Killegrew.

Thomas Killegrew had already written plays before the closing of the theatres, and had been at Court as a Page of Honour to Charles I and had become a firm favourite of the King. He followed Prince Charles into exile and became "Our trusty and well beloved" and "one of the Grooms of Our Bedchamber"—to quote the King's own words in his Charter. At the Restoration Killegrew returned with the Court on May 23rd, 1660. While in exile he had also been appointed Master of the Revels; but the office was claimed by Sir Henry Herbert, and as we have said, the problems which arose out of this were eventually resolved—on Herbert's death Killegrew officially assumed the title.

These men, Davenant and Killegrew, were the two into whose hands fell the task of establishing the theatre in London. This task was fraught with many difficulties, division of the repertoire and engagement of actors, and all the many intricacies of theatrical management.

Arrangements had also to be made to bring the other Managers, who had so quickly taken the opportunity to re-open and had continued to play, under the control of the Patentees, and this took some years to accomplish. The two Patents were ratified in 1662, giving Davenant permission to build a theatre, and styled his Company "the Servants of Our dearly-beloved brother James, Duke of York"; and Killegrew also to build a theatre and to call his Company "the King's Servants." Both Companies were granted Royal Liveries. Before arrangements for the new playhouses were ready, Killegrew had opened at Gibbons' Tennis Court in Vere Street, converted temporarily into a "Theatre Royal," as early as November 8th, 1660, with a Company of the old actors. Davenant opened at the Salisbury Court playhouse a few days later,

on November 15th, with the young Betterton as his leading actor.

In June 1661 Davenant moved to Lincoln's Inn Fields, converting Lisle's Tennis Court into the first Duke's Theatre, said to be the first theatre to have a Proscenium and to use scenery which was "set" and "struck." Here his Company acted until the new Duke's Theatre in Dorset Gardens was build in 1671. Meantime Killegrew was busy with his plans for a new Theatre Royal. This was built in a field reached by a pathway from Drury Lane to Bridges Street (now called Catherine Street), and was known as "The Theatre Royal, Bridges Street," though soon to be simply called "Drury Lane." The theatre was opened May 7th, 1663, with a play by Beaumont and Fletcher, *The Humorous Lieutenant*.

As we have seen, the actors from pre-Restoration days had formed the nucleus of the re-formed companies. The erstwhile Boy actors like Kynaston, now grown into men, carried on the Elizabethan tradition; but the greatest change was about to take place. In Italy women had begun to appear on the public stage as early as 1565. The custom spread to other European countries. Travellers reported on what they had seen, but England remained, as always, bound by tradition. It is recorded that a visiting French company at the Blackfriars Theatre in 1629 contained an actress; an eye-witness reports: "Glad am I to say that they were hissed, hooted, and pippin-pelted from the stage; so that I do not think they will soon be ready to try the same again." The Company retired to France in the face of the "Puritan" disapproval.

The experiment was not again made until the private production of Davenant's *The Siege of Rhodes* in 1656, when a Mrs. Coleman, the wife of the composer of the music of the "opera," played Ianthe. Though not a professional actress, she is the first known Englishwoman to appear on a stage. The exiled King Charles had naturally grown used to actresses appearing in plays in France, and besides his love for the Theatre it must be admitted he had, judging from his future "raids" upon the playhouse, an eye for a pretty actress. So what more natural than that he should stipulate in the Charter he gave to Killegrew, which is still in existence, that women should take the Stage:—

"And for as much as many playes formerly acted doe containe severall prophane, obscene and scurrilous passages, and the women's part therein have byn acted by men in the habit of women, at which some have taken offence, for the preventing of these abuses for the future, wee doe hereby strictly commande and enjoyne, that from henceforth noe new play shall be acted by either of the said companies conteyning anie passages offensive to pietie or good manners, nor any old or revived play conteyning any such offensive passages as aforesaid, untill the same shall be corrected and purged by the said masters or governors of the said respective companies from all such offensive and scandalous passages as aforesaid: And wee doe likewise permit and give leave that all the woemen's part to be acted in either of the said two companies for the time to come may be performed by woemen so long as their recreacones, which by reason of the abuse aforesaid were scandalous and offensive, may by such reformation be esteemed not onely harmless delight, but useful and instructive representations of humane life, to such of our good subjects as shall resort to the same". . . .

It must be remembered that Puritan tendencies among the people still existed—so to get his way and not to seem to be offending his subjects, he cleverly chose his words to appear as though he were protecting their morals by removing the Boy actors and indulging in a campaign for the purification of the Stage!

To whom fell the honour of being the first English professional actress has often been disputed. It is known that she appeared at the Vere Street Theatre on December 3rd, 1660, as Desdemona in *The Moor of Venice*—an adaptation of *Othello*. A Prologue to the play announced:

"I come, unknown to any of the rest,
To tell you news—I saw the Lady drest;
The Woman playes to-day, mistake me not,
No Man in Gown, or Page in Petty-Coat;
A Woman to my knowledge. . . ."

Though the claims of several ladies who later became established actresses to be this Desdemona have been put forward, John Downes, who was Prompter with Davenant's Company for many years, states in his book *Roscius Anglicanus* that it was Margaret Hughes. This book of theatre notes, published in 1708, is one of our chief sources of information on the early Restoration stage.

It was still some years before women became completely established in the theatre as time was needed for their training; till then, the parts were played by actors.

Of these early Companies many names stand out in the history of the stage: Thomas Betterton and Henry Harris at the Duke's Theatre; Michael Mohun and Charles Hart at the King's; James Nokes, John Lacy and Cave Underhill are recorded as the best comedians of the day, and often referred to in the pages of Pepys' Diary, to which we owe so much of the backstage tittle-tattle of the day.

As the actresses came to the fore, it is the names of Nell Gwynn, Mary Davis, Elizabeth Barry and Ann Bracegirdle which stand out—often, it must be said, for the tales of their off-stage life as much as for their professional careers. Betterton's wife, Mary Sanderson, is almost alone in her reputation for virtue!

The plays of the Restoration era and their writers are a study on their own. They produced a style of Comedy of Manners which vividly reflected the fashionable life of the period and was eminently suited to the aristocratic audiences who frequented the playhouse.

The playwright and wit, it must be remembered, did not really take himself seriously or regard his work as anything more than a kind of social accomplishment. The dazzling brilliance of their dialogue and the amoral machinations of their plots remain as fresh today as when they were written.

The Elizabethan dramatists were revised and rewritten to suit the new style of playhouse and the changed tastes. These revisions, particularly of Shakespeare, were to remain in vogue for many years.

Puritanism was again to raise its ugly head with the publication of Jeremy Collier's *Short View of the Profaneness and Immorality of the English Stage* in 1698; but this time it came from a Tory and a high Churchman.

The trends of the day went away from the moral freedom of the early Restoration times, and as we reach the days of Queen Anne a new upper-middle class audience joined the aristocratic frequenters of the theatre, who before had looked on the playhouse as a kind of Club. A new style of Moral play and a pseudo-Classic drama, often masking a political tract, was evoked.

The first Drury Lane Theatre was burnt down in 1672, the Company using the now disused playhouse in Lincoln's Inn, as the Duke's men had gone to Dorset Garden. The new theatre, designed by Sir Christopher Wren, was opened in 1674. Trouble ensued between the two Companies—actors deserted one for the other. Audiences favouring one house more than the other caused financial difficulties. Killegrew gave up in favour of his son Charles, and the affairs of Drury Lane went from bad to worse. At Dorset Garden things were not much better; there Davenant's widow and son with Betterton were in charge. A union of the two houses was proposed by Hart and Kynaston. This was achieved and the Lane was opened in 1682 as the sole Patent Theatre in London, with Betterton as the leading actor.

Peace did not long reign. By 1690 the Davenant Patent was sold to Christopher Rich. Some of the Company revolted and left with Betterton to open the playhouse again in Lincoln's Inn Fields in 1695, going to the new Queen's Theatre built by Vanbrugh in the Haymarket in 1705; Betterton retired in 1709.

The affairs of theatreland remained in rivalry and chaos, and eventually Rich was turned out of Drury Lane and control ultimately passed into the hands of Cibber, Doggett and Wilks in 1711 working under Killegrew's Patent as a united Company for the Drama, leaving the Queen's Theatre to become an Opera House. Doggett was replaced by Barton Booth in 1713 and under the Triumvirate the theatre passed into one of the most prosperous periods in its history.

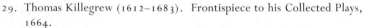

29. Thomas Killegrew (1612–1683). Frontispiece to his Collected Plays, 1664.

30. Sir William Davenant (1606–1668). Frontispiece to his Collected Works, 1673.

31. The Charter granted by Charles II to Thomas Killegrew in 1662, the Patent under which the Theatre Royal, Drury Lane, was founded. This Charter, the second obtained by Killegrew, on April 25th, made his proposed new theatre the "Theatre Royal" and his company "The King's Servants." The theatre was opened on May 7th, 1663, with Beaumont and Fletcher's, *The Humorous Lieutenant*.

This original document, which has changed hands many times and for sums ranging from £30,000 to 10/–, has been lost and found again, and must still be held by whoever owns Drury Lane Theatre. The present company has held it since 1897, and it is reproduced by their kind permission.

The original warrant of 1660 had expressly provided that actresses could replace the boy actors, and it was at the Vere Street Theatre, on December 8th, that Desdemona was first played by a woman, who is thought to have been Margaret Hughes.

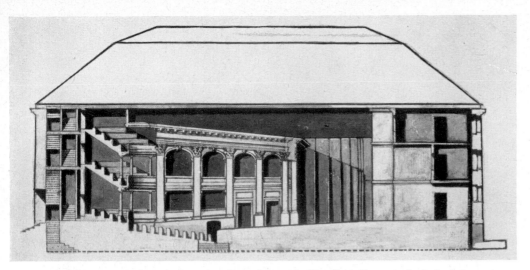

From the earliest times theatres announced performances by a bill set up on a post outside. (Hence the later term "Poster.") The earliest extant is 15″ × 9″ (No. 34). Early bills announced only the title of the play. Later, they became smaller and the names of the actors were added, and still later their roles. Garrick was the first to achieve larger type than his colleagues, starting jealousy over "billing," which still persists.

The playbills served the double purpose of Announcement and "Programme," though this word did not become current till the mid-nineteenth century, when playbills had grown to vast proportions, and the Programme, as we know it, developed.

32. Design by Sir Christopher Wren now in the Library of All Souls College, Oxford, for a Restoration Theatre, probably the second Theatre Royal, Drury Lane, opened September 15th, 1674. This replaced the first theatre, built in 1663 and burned down in 1672.

No pictures exist of the first theatre, and only the doubtful Wren drawing of the second shows it as it originally appeared, though a few unspecified engravings (as No. 33 below) can safely be said to represent something of the interior. This theatre, with alterations and redecorations, remained until its demolition in 1792.

34. The earliest regular theatre Playbill in existence, for a performance at Drury Lane in 1685. From the original in the Public Record Office.

33. Joe Haines, comedian (d. 1701).

Joe Haines, a famous comedian and a great practical joker; shown here speaking the Epilogue (which he delivered seated on an ass) to *The Unhappy Kindness*, at Drury Lane in 1697. This play, by Thomas Scott, was an adaptation of Beaumont and Fletcher's *Wife for a Month*. It is a Frontispiece to Thomas Brown's works, 1719. Brown, a miscellaneous writer of plays, prologues and epilogues, was the first to introduce political satire to the stage, a form of play that was to be the cause of the introduction of censorship, under the Lord Chamberlain's jurisdiction, in 1737, when Sir Robert Walpole objected to the satires of Fielding.

35. Exterior of the Duke's Theatre, Dorset Garden, 1673.

36. Interior of the Duke's Theatre, Dorset Garden, 1673.

The Dorset Garden Theatre, opened 1671. This was the second Duke's Theatre, the first being the conversion of Lisle's Tennis Court into the Duke's Theatre, Lincoln's Inn Fields, by Davenant in 1661; it reverted to a tennis court after the new theatre in Dorset Gardens was built. This was the second theatre to be erected in this district. The first, in Salisbury Court, built in 1629, was an indoor theatre and was used surreptitiously during the Commonwealth. After the Restoration it was in use till it was destroyed in the Fire of London, 1666.

Davenant built his new theatre nearer the river. It was designed by Sir Christopher Wren and exceeded Drury Lane in size. Unfortunately Davenant died before it was finished, but his widow and son with Betterton, their leading actor, carried the work to its completion. It was here that Elkanah Settles' tragedy *The Emperor of Morocco* was produced in 1673, with Mary Betterton as the Empress Laula, and Betterton as Crimalhaz. It is probably the first play to have a series of plates, which also show the exterior and proscenium of the theatre and give an impression of the staging at this date.

37. Interior of the Duke's Theatre, Dorset Garden, 1673.

38. Edward Kynaston (c. 1640–1706), one of the last of the boy players of female roles. Pepys said of him, "He made the loveliest Lady that I ever saw."

39. Margaret Hughes (1643–1719). Probably the first actress to appear on the public stage; playing Desdemona in *The Moor of Venice*, Killegrew's version of *Othello*, 1660.

40. Mary Davis. Actress at Lincoln's Inn Fields Theatre (fl. 1663–1668), and a mistress of Charles II.

41. Eleanor Gwynn (1650–1687), actress at Drury Lane from 1665 and became mistress of Charles II.

42. William Harris, as the Empress of Morocco in Thomas Duffett's Burlesque, Drury Lane, 1673.

43. Thomas Betterton, actor and manager (1635–1710). His wife was Mary Sanderson, the actress.

HAMPTON COURT PALACE

MAGDALEN COLLEGE, OXFORD

44. John Lacey (1622–1681), as Teague in *The Committee*, Scruple in *The Cheats* and Galliard in *The Variety*. Triple portrait by Michael Wright, c. 1665.

45. Henry Harris (1634?–1704), as Cardinal Wolsey, 1663. From a pastel by John Greenhill. He played in *Henry VIII* with Davenant's Company at Lincoln's Inn Fields Theatre.

46. John Dryden (1631–1700), poet and dramatist. He first wrote for the theatre in 1664 (*The Indian Queen*). Among his large output of some thirty plays are: *The Conquest of Granada* (1670), *Marriage à la Mode* (1671), *All For Love* (1677) and *The Spanish Friar* (1679).

47. Thomas Otway (1652–1685), dramatist. First appeared, unsuccessfully, as an actor in 1670, turned to play-writing and wrote some nine plays, which include *The Orphan* (1680), *The Soldier's Fortune* (1681) and *Venice Preserv'd* (1682).

48. Nicholas Rowe (1674–1718), dramatist, wrote seven tragedies, among the most famous of which are: *Tamerlane* (1701), *The Fair Penitent* (1703), *Jane Shore* (1714), *Lady Jane Grey* (1715). He edited the plays of Shakespeare in 1709.

49. William Wycherley (1640–1716), dramatist. Famous for his bawdy Comedies of Manners. His five plays include: *The Gentleman Dancing Master* (1672), *The Country Wife* (1675) and *The Plain Dealer* (1676). The plays, though coarse and indecent, attack the vices of the day; causing him to be called "a moralist at heart."

50. Susannah Centlivre (1667–1723), actress and dramatist. Though she was never more than a country actress, as a dramatist she contributed some nineteen plays to the theatre, from 1700, among which are: *The Busy Body* (1709), *The Perplex'd Lovers* (1712), *The Wonder* (1714) and *A Bold Stroke for a Wife* (1718).

51. George Farquhar (1678–1707), dramatist. Commenced his career as an actor but achieved fame with his Comedies of Manners, which include: *The Constant Couple* (1699), *The Inconstant* (1702), *The Recruiting Officer* (1706) and *The Beaux Stratagem* (1707).

52. William Congreve (1670–1729), dramatist. Most brilliant exponent of the Comedies of Manners. His first play, *The Old Batchelor* (1693), brought him instant success. Among his other plays are: *The Double Dealer* (1694), *Love for Love* (1695), *The Mourning Bride* (1697) and *The Way of the World* (1700). In 1707 he was for a short time in management with Vanbrugh at the Queen's Theatre, presenting operas.

53. Aphra Behn (1640–1689), the first woman dramatist. Her first play to be produced was *The Forc'd Marriage* (1671). She also wrote some seventeen plays, notable for their coarse exuberance, even in a licentious age. She had an adventurous career as a Government agent in the Low Countries, before turning to the theatre, where her work is as full of wit and amorous intrigue as she was herself.

54. Sir John Vanbrugh (1664–1726), dramatist and architect. He built the Queen's Theatre in the Haymarket (1705) (later to become an opera house), which opened with his play, *The Confederacy*. His other plays include: *The Relapse* (1697), *The Provok'd Wife* (1697). His work as an architect caused him to leave the theatre and his last unfinished play was completed by Colley Cibber in 1728 as *The Provok'd Husband*.

55. Anthony Leigh (d. 1692), as Father Dominic in Dryden's *The Spanish Friar*, Dorset Garden, 1679.

56. Colley Cibber (1671–1757) as Lord Foppington in Vanbrugh's *The Relapse*, Drury Lane, 1697.

57. Barton Booth, actor (1681–1733). First appeared in London, 1700. His association with Drury Lane lasted from 1708 to 1728.

58. Thomas Southerne, dramatist (1660–1746). Wrote, amongst other plays, *The Fatal Marriage* (1694), *Oroonoko* (1695).

59. Elizabeth Barry, actress (1653–1713). Created Isabella in Southerne's *Fatal Marriage*, and Belvidera in Otway's *Venice Preserv'd*.

60. Anne Bracegirdle (1663?–1743), as Semerina in Aphra Behn's *The Widow Ranter*, Drury Lane, 1689. She created Angelica in Congreve's *Love for Love*, Millamant in *The Way of the World*. She retired in 1707, piqued by the success of Anne Oldfield, only to reappear in *Love for Love* at Betterton's Farewell in 1709. She was as much esteemed for the austerity of her private life as for the excellence of her acting.

61. Anne Oldfield, actress (1683–1730). Made her first success in Cibber's *Careless Husband*, 1703. From then on her career was one of unbroken triumph. Though she created Marcia in Joseph Addison's *Cato* (1713), and Rowe's Jane Shore (1714), it was in comedy that she excelled, creating Mrs. Sullen in Farquhar's *Beaux Stratagem* (1707) and Lady Townley in Cibber's *The Provok'd Husband* (1727).

62. *Troilus and Cressida, 1709.*

63. *Henry VIII, 1709.*

Nicholas Rowe, the dramatist, added stage directions, and in certain cases, act and scene divisions into his edition of Shakespeare's plays. Published in 1709, it contains a frontispiece to each play, constituting the first illustrations to Shakespeare. Many of them are undoubtedly founded on contemporary staging—the theatrical conventions of the day are strictly adhered to. In *Troilus and Cressida*, though the actors wear stage Classical costumes, the Cressida remains little removed from her period, but for the plumes traditionally worn in tragedy. In *Henry VIII*, though the King and the Cardinal are, as was usual, correctly dressed, the Courtiers remain strictly of their own day. *The Taming of the Shrew* is shown as an entirely contemporary comedy, in "Modern Dress." Hamlet, said to represent Betterton, is in the strict methods of presentation which held the stage until 1783. The overturned chair (on the appearance of the Ghost) is a piece of stage business referred to in reports on Garrick, and depicted in two paintings in the Garrick Club Collection, one of Spranger Barry c. 1752 and another dating from about 1776. In 1777 Henderson was brought to task by critics for omitting what was called "the established custom."

64. *The Taming of the Shrew, 1709.*

65. *Hamlet, 1709.*

66. Lincoln's Inn Fields Theatre as it was in 1811.

The first Lincoln's Inn Fields Theatre lasted 1661–1671. It was later used by Betterton from 1695–1705. Christopher Rich, forced from Drury Lane in 1711, planned to move to Lincoln's Inn. He died before the new theatre was opened in 1714, succeeded by his son John who remained there until 1732, when he went to Covent Garden. The building, last used as a theatre in 1743, was finally demolished in 1848. (The picture shows it as it appeared in 1811, when it had become a warehouse.) It is not certain that both Lincoln's Inn theatres occupied the same site.

67. Robert Wilks (1665–1732) as Sir Harry Wildair in Farquhar's *The Constant Couple*—the part he created at Drury Lane in 1699.

68. Cave Underhill (1634–1710?) as Obadiah in Robert Howard's *The Committee*, Drury Lane, 1665.

69. David Garrick as Ranger and Hannah Pritchard as Clarinda in Dr. Benjamin Hoadly's *The Suspicious Husband*, Covent Garden, 1747, from a painting by Francis Hayman.

PART THREE

Georgian

(1714–1811)

WE now enter upon an era which is to cover nearly a century and embrace some of the most vital changes in theatre history. The first great actor-manager is to come and go; costume is to change from being fundamentally contemporary into the realms of the theatrical mock-historical; scenic and lighting developments are to appear; playhouse reforms are to take place, and by the end a new stage dynasty is to arrive.

In 1714 the new younger generation of actors was in sole charge of the Drama at Drury Lane. Foremost among the actresses was Anne Oldfield. Booth and Cibber shared the male acting honours, and for the next twenty years the theatre enjoyed an almost uninterrupted prosperity. Much of the story of these days and those immediately preceding them is told by Cibber in the famous Apology for His Life, the first great theatrical autobiography.

Drury Lane was not for long the only theatre in London. The dispossessed Christopher Rich went on to build himself a new theatre in Lincoln's Inn. He died before it was completed, and his son John carried on the work. It was opened in December 1714, claiming to operate under Davenant's Patent.

Rich had a taste for acting but was coarse and devoid of any education; but his dramatic genius was responsible for the introduction of pantomime to this country in 1717. It was as Lun the silent Harlequin that he achieved fame, forcing his rivals at Drury Lane to embark on similar pantomimes by 1723. Both houses prospered, though again in continuous rivalry. It was Rich who found *The Beggar's Opera* in 1727, crowding his house for 62 nights.

James Quin joined Rich in 1717 and quickly established himself as a leading actor.

The practice of allowing privileged spectators to sit upon the stage during performances led to a serious riot of a kind which was to break out many times in the ensuing years.

One night, in a principal scene of *Macbeth*, a nobleman crossed from one side of the stage to the other, in front of the actors, to speak to a friend; when Rich remonstrated with him upon the impropriety of such behaviour my lord struck him in the face. Rich and Quin drew their swords, the rest of the company supported them, and the beaux took the offender's side. But the players proving too strong, their foes were driven out of the theatre. Reinforced, the rioters soon returned, smashed the handsome mirrors that lined the proscenium, threw torches among the scenery, tore up the seats, and it was not until the military were called out that the disturbance was quelled.

In 1731 Rich decided to build a new theatre in Covent Garden, which was opened on December 7th, 1732. Here Quin reigned as leading man and Rich produced his Pantomimes . . . a period said to be a dead level of conventional dullness and mediocrity unbroken until the arrival of Peg Woffington in 1740.

At Drury Lane now, with a formidable rival on its doorstep, they continued to prosper, though in an uneventful way. Wilks died in 1732: Booth, who had returned in 1728, died in 1733, leaving Cibber in sole possession, and he too sold his share and retired, leaving his son Theophilus at the Lane. The shares in the Patent, after a revolt led by young Cibber and several changes of hands, passed to Charles Fleetwood—a spendthrift, gambler and a man utterly devoid of honesty and honour, always deeply in debt; the theatre under his direction sank to a low level. It was not until the arrival of Charles Macklin, who at Lincoln's Inn had been experimenting with a more natural style of acting, that the fortune of the Lane increased. Macklin decided to act *The Merchant of Venice* as Shakespeare wrote it, disgarding the Lord Lansdown version, *The Jew of Venice*, which for forty years had held the stage. He wished to play Shylock as a tragic character, dispensing with the red wig and the comedy portrayal of the role. Despite the wishes of Fleetwood he made his experiment in January 1741 and took the Town by storm. It was the first blow to the old school of acting, as represented by Quin, following in Betterton's footsteps.

In 1720 a Little theatre in the Haymarket was opened almost opposite the Queen's Theatre—then the Opera House. At first a French Company was engaged, but the venture was not successful. It was then used for diverse entertainments as it could only obtain temporary licences and open on the sufferance of the Patent Theatres. In 1730 Henry Fielding took the theatre and produced his famous burlesque *Tom Thumb*. The house was used by the Rebels from Drury Lane in 1733, and Fielding continued to produce his political satires there, these and other similar plays eventually arousing the wrath of Sir Robert Walpole, who brought in the Licensing Act of 1737 which introduced Censorship and confirmed the monopoly of Drury Lane and Covent Garden, under the jurisdiction of the Lord Chamberlain.

Another theatre which had sprung up on the outskirts of London at Whitechapel was in Ayliff Street,

Goodmans Fields. This was run by Henry Giffard, who on the passing of the Licensing Act evaded its restrictions by issuing tickets for a Concert and performing a play "gratis" between the two parts; he was unmolested, the Patent Theatres no doubt thinking him too remote to be a menace to their Monopoly. It was here that David Garrick made his first London appearance on October 9th, 1741, as Richard III. He, like Macklin, had new ideas about acting. His debut was sensational. Soon all fashionable London flocked to Goodmans Fields to see him in many parts until May 1741 when the Patent Theatres, alarmed at the loss of their audiences, invoked the new Act and closed the theatre. Garrick negotiated an engagement with Fleetwood who had been quicker than Rich to seize upon this new attraction, and so on May 11th, 1742, Garrick entered Drury Lane, which was soon to become his home for the rest of his career, a new era in theatrical history was about to commence.

Before the way could be opened for this new era, much had to be cleared away. Fleetwood faced a revolt of his Company, and finally his financial difficulties forced him from the Lane. Control fell into the hands of two City men, Green and Amber, who asked James Lacy to undertake the management. This he did, in 1744, but the way was not clear yet. Though Garrick was drawing full houses, it was not until 1747, after he had been at Covent Garden for a season, that he and Lacy together became complete owners of the Patent and rulers of Drury Lane.

The new regime opened on September 15th, 1747, and Garrick spoke a Prologue by Samuel Johnson, which has become famous in theatre annals. In this he said:—

"Hard is his lot, that here by fortune plac'd
Must watch the wild vicissitude of taste
With every meteor of caprice must play
And chance the new blown bubbles of the day.
Ah, let not censure term our fate our choice,
The stage but echoes back the public voice,
The drama's laws, the drama's patrons give
For we that live to please, must please to live.
Then prompt no more the follies you decry,
As tyrants doom their tools of guilt to die;
'Tis yours, this night, to bid the reign commence
Of rescued nature, and reviving sense;
To chace the charm of sound, the pomp of show
For useful mirth and salutary woe
Bid scenic virtue form the rising age
And truth diffuse her radiance from the stage."

The opening play was *The Merchant of Venice*, with Macklin as Shylock. Garrick gathered round him a fine company: Mrs. Pritchard, Peg Woffington, Kitty Clive, Mrs. Cibber, Henry Woodward and Spranger Barry. Doctor Arne was the Director of Music. Garrick was swift to institute reforms, both before and behind the curtain. He insisted on strict rehearsals for the Company and began to pay much attention to the "business" of the scene, which in modern language means he devoted time to Production, not leaving things to chance or the traditions and whims of the actors.

As we have already seen, playgoers' manners were bad. A playbill in October 1747 bore the Note: "As the admittance of persons behind the scenes has occasioned a general complaint on account of the frequent interruption in the performance, it is hoped that gentlemen won't be offended that no money will be taken there for the future." At first this attempt to remove spectators from the stage was not completely successful, but eventually Garrick's will prevailed.

The entertainments produced at the theatre had lengthened to include both a Tragedy and a Comedy, often with other items. It had become the custom to admit the audience at half price for the third Act of the Tragedy. This also Garrick tried to abolish, resulting in riots both at Drury Lane and Covent Garden in 1763. This system was to remain for many years. It was still the custom at the Haymarket until 1873.

Garrick altered the times of playing, turning theatre-going into a completely evening pursuit. He began moves to reform the dressing of plays, but though not completely abolishing the wearing of contemporary clothes, he introduced more correct historical authenticity and period into the dress of leading parts. His visits to France, where he was extremely popular, introduced him to new experiments with lighting and scenery, which with the help of De Loutherbourg, his scene designer, he brought to the Lane. It must be remembered that the auditorium as well as the stage, was completely lit during performances; though Garrick attempted to focus his lighting towards the actors, it was many years before the auditorium lights were dimmed during the performance.

At Covent Garden Quin still carried on in the old methods, but was succeeded by Spranger Barry who had shared the leading parts with Garrick at the Lane. This caused a period of acute rivalry. In 1750 Barry, with Mrs. Cibber, who had joined him, acted *Romeo and Juliet*. The same night Garrick acted the part with George Anne Bellamy at Drury Lane. They also vied with each other in *Lear* and *Othello*.

Rich was still famous for his pantomimes, so Garrick, who had originally intended to avoid such entertainments, was forced to follow suit, and promptly began to beat Rich on his own ground.

Garrick wrote plays and was responsible for new versions of Shakespeare, then thought to be improvements on the Restoration texts; but to our eyes they seem just as curious. He was honoured by continued Royal Visits to the theatre, while he enlarged and redecorated in 1762 and again in 1775.

The first sound of the name which was to dominate the whole London theatrical world was heard on December 29th, 1775, when Mrs. Siddons, who as Sarah Kemble had begun with her family to make a provincial reputation, made her London debut as Portia; her season was not a success and she retired back to the Provinces. The day of the Kembles had not yet come.

Garrick decided to retire in 1776, made his Farewell on June 10th, and the most glorious epoch in the history of the Old Drury drew to a close. At Covent Garden, control had passed to Rich's son-in-law, John Beard, and later to Henry Harris. It was here that the first step towards a new style of play was made with the production of Goldsmith's *She Stoops to Conquer* in 1773.

The plays of the era had been mainly the old repertory, revised to suit the taste of the day, with the addition of many slight comedies, and though popular at the time proved of little permanent worth. Any new tragedies were mostly written in the old bombastic style handed down from the early days of the century. Arthur Murphy and George Coleman the Elder are the names who stand out for the most originality of thought, until Goldsmith paved the way for the return of the Comedy of Manners through the work of Sheridan.

Richard Brinsley Sheridan, whose father was an actor and manager of a Dublin theatre, bought half of Garrick's share of Drury Lane in 1776, in partnership with his father-in-law Thomas Linley. Two years later he acquired Lacy's share. The main feature of the early part of his era is his own plays. There was no actor fit to succeed Garrick, though it was hoped that John Henderson would so do; but his early death in 1785 left the way open for the rise of John Philip Kemble.

In October 1782, Mrs. Siddons returned to the Lane in triumph. In September 1783, Kemble made his first appearance in London, acting Hamlet for the first time in a costume of a theatrical Elizabethan mode—and contemporary dress in Shakespeare was abolished from the stage. Kemble became actor-manager of the Lane in 1788. Sheridan completely rebuilt the old theatre and re-opened in 1794. Kemble remained with him until 1802, when he left to join Harris at Covent Garden. Here he remained through the destruction of the old theatre by fire, facing the O.P. Riots at the new theatre in 1809, retiring in 1817 after 29 years of management. His achievements we will meet in the next period.

The tastes of the day had changed; the audiences were demanding spectacle and lavish production. The new large theatre required these and a broader method of oratory. Melodrama was introduced from France in 1802 at Covent Garden. The jaded public clamoured more and more for new attractions. Sheridan introduced water, animals, performing and otherwise, into his theatre. The craze for Master Betty came and went; only the Kembles upheld what was the real legitimate drama, though forced to adapt it to suit the public demands and the box office.

70. Hamlet: the Play scene. An engraving published 1730. Probably depicts Robert Wilks at Drury Lane.

THEATRE ROYAL
April a Comedy with the Mock Doctor
For the Benefit of the Author of the Farce

71. A Benefit Ticket, engraved by William Hogarth, for Henry Fielding's *The Mock Doctor*, Drury Lane, 1732.

72. Benjamin Griffin (1680–1740) and Benjamin Johnson (1665?–1742) as Ananias and Tribulation in Ben Jonson's *The Alchymist*, Drury Lane, 1738. This play, written in 1610 and *Valpone*, 1606, are his most famous plays.

73. Charles Fleetwood, Manager of Drury Lane, 1734–1745. Represented as *Sir Fopling Arrested*—a reference to his constant financial troubles. (Sir Fopling Flutter is a character in George Etheridge's *Man of Mode*.)

Christopher Rich, a lawyer, had bought Davenant's share of the Royal Patent from his son, and he gained control at Drury Lane in 1693. He remained there until 1711 when he was removed, leaving Cibber in control with Killegrew's Patent. He did not live to see his new theatre in Lincoln's Inn Fields completed. His son John carried on successfully there, introducing Pantomime into this country, with himself as Harlequin.

In 1732 John Rich built a new theatre in Covent Garden, operating under Davenant's Patent. Thus began the rivalry of the two great theatres, which gained between them the sole right of performing drama, until their monopoly was finally broken in 1843. Rich was succeeded on his death by his son-in-law John Beard. The theatre and Patent were sold in 1767. After difficulties, George Coleman the Elder became sole manager until 1774 when the theatre passed to Thomas Harris, and eventually into the control of John Philip Kemble.

The theatre was reconstructed in 1778 and yet again in 1792. It was burnt down in 1808.

77. Satirical engraving, *The Stage Mutiny*, April 1733. Theophilus Cibber led a revolt against the management of Drury Lane, which had fallen into unprofessional hands, and with some of the Company set up on his own at the Little Theatre in the Haymarket, where they acted until they were forced to return at the end of the year. The picture shows Cibber (as Pistol), centre, surrounded by the Company (*L.* to *R.*): William Milward, Benjamin Griffin, John Harper (as Falstaff), Mary Heron and William Mills. John Highmore, a Patentee of Drury Lane, exhibits a scroll, on which is the cost of his controlling interest. He is supported by Ellis, the Manager, and the widow and daughter of Robert Wilks, the actor and part owner of the theatre, who had just died. Old Colley Cibber, who had sold his share to Highmore, sits in the corner, with the money bags.

78. Lavinia Fenton (1708–1760). Made a successful début in 1726, but retired two years later to become the mistress of the Duke of Bolton, whom she later married. Though she appeared in plays, it is as Polly in the first production of *The Beggars' Opera* in 1728 that she is still remembered.

79. Charlotte Charke (1713–1760). Actress, daughter of Colley Cibber. Her early unsuccessful marriage to a violinist, Richard Charke, caused her to go on the stage in 1730. She later became keeper of a grocery store, manageress of a puppet show, a valet (in male attire), a sausage-seller and a publican.

80. Theophilus Cibber (1703–1758), son of Colley Cibber, as Pistol in *Henry IV, Part 2*, Drury Lane, 1729.

81. Catherine Clive (1711–1785). Made her début at Drury Lane in 1728 under her maiden name of Raftor. She quickly achieved success as a singer and actress. She remained at Drury Lane till 1743, creating Nell in Charles Coffey's *The Devil to Pay* (1731), Lappett in Fielding's *The Miser* (1733), and playing many other famous parts in Comedy, including Millamant in *The Way of the World*, Miss Prue in *Love for Love*, Miss Hoyden in *The Relapse*. She also played Shakespeare's Desdemona, Celia, Olivia and Portia.

Though she achieved fame as a comedienne, her ambition was to play tragedy, for which she was unsuitable.

After a spell at Covent Garden she returned to Drury Lane when Garrick assumed management. She remained with him until her retirement in 1769. During this period she was the original Kitty in James Townley's *High Life Below Stairs* (1759), Muslin in Arthur Murphy's *The Way to Keep Him* (1760), Lady Freelove in George Coleman's *The Jealous Wife* and Mrs. Heidelberg in Garrick and Coleman's *The Clandestine Marriage* (1766).

82. Catherine Clive as Mrs. Riot, the Fine Lady in *Lethe*, Drury Lane, 1749. David Garrick wrote his first play, a dramatic satire, before he went on the stage. It was produced at Drury Lane in 1740. In the first version there was no part of the Fine Lady, though Kitty Clive was in the cast as Miss Lucy (a character omitted later). When the play was re-written and revised in 1749, the Fine Lady made her first appearance. To keep the satire topical, the play was again revised in 1756, when Garrick added the part of Lord Chalkstone for himself.

It was as the Fine Lady that Kitty Clive chose to make her farewell to the stage at Drury Lane in 1769. She was then sixty-two. Garrick, at fifty-two, whom she requested to play Don Felix in *The Wonder*, had doubts about their playing these parts at their ages. Mrs. Clive wrote to him: "What signifies fifty-two? They had rather see The Garrick and The Clive at a hundred and four, than any of the Moderns—the Ancients, you know, have always been admired."

83. Margaret Woffington (1714?–1760), speaking an Epilogue "in the habit of a Volunteer reading the Gazette containing an Account of the late Action at Falkirk." Delivered after a performance of Beaumont and Fletcher's *The Scornful Lady* at Drury Lane, 1746.

Peg Woffington made her London début at Covent Garden in 1730. She quickly became famous in breeches parts. Her Sir Harry Wildair in *The Constant Couple* became the toast of the town. She excelled also as Millamant. She also played tragedy, creating the part of Lady Randolph in William Home's *Douglas* in 1757.

She was notorious for her quarrels with other leading actresses of her day—Kitty Clive, Mrs. Cibber and George Anne Bellamy. The latter she is said to have wounded with a dagger in a fit of rage.

84. Margaret Woffington as Mistress Page in *The Merry Wives of Windsor*, Drury Lane, 1743. Her other Shakespearean parts include Portia, and Isabella in *Measure for Measure*. It was as Rosalind that she made her last appearance at Drury Lane in 1757, at a Benefit for the lesser members of the Company. She broke down at the commencement of the Epilogue and was unable to conclude. She lingered on in ill-health till she died at Twickenham in 1760.

85. Scene from *Henry IV, Part I*. This engraving, dated 1743, of a painting by Francis Hayman for Vauxhall Gardens—possibly depicting James Quin (1693–1766) in his most famous part—cannot with certainty be said to be of a theatrical performance. He returned after his retirement to play Falstaff in 1752 and 1753.

86. James Quin as Coriolanus in James Thompson's play, Covent Garden, 1749. This engraving shows the old style of Tragedy costume, which Quin still retained—the plumes, peruke and spreading shape. On its first production Volumnia was played by George Anne Bellamy and Vetunia by Peg Woffington. Genest says it was acted ten times "but when compared with Shakespeare's, it is regular, cold and declamatory."

Quin made his London début at Drury Lane in 1714. He was at Lincoln's Inn Fields for fourteen years, returning to Drury Lane until he retired in 1751. He was the leading actor of his day—the last supporter of the old school of Betterton—until the rise of Garrick, whom he strongly resented for his new methods, of whom he said: "if the young fellow is right, I and the rest of the players have been all wrong."

87. The "Laughing Audience," by Hogarth, c. 1748. A playhouse scene, showing the Orange Girls, who also provided the audience with the "Bill of the Play."

88. Joseph Miller (1684–1738) as Teague in *The Committee*, Drury Lane, 1738. His most famous part, which he played from 1709. He is best remembered for the Jest Book published under his name, the year after he died.

The system of paying actors by a salary and the proceeds of a Benefit performance appears to date from the beginning of the eighteenth century. Elizabeth Barry had been ordered a Benefit by James II, and what commenced as a compliment passed into a custom. Actors became dependent on their popularity and social connections for a substantial part of their income. They had the task, often humiliating, of selling tickets to friends and patrons. Playwrights received their first Benefit on the third night, if their play achieved this mark of success. Payment by royalties did not come until 1860. Special tickets were sometimes designed. This system had more or less died out in London by the 1850's, except in a few special cases.

89. Ticket engraved by Hogarth for Joe Miller's Benefit: Congreve's *The Old Batchelor* at Drury Lane. October 3rd, 1734.

90. David Garrick (1717–1779). The earliest engraved portrait, 1745, from a painting by Arthur Pond.

91. David Garrick as Richard III in Cibber's version of Shakespeare's play, Drury Lane, 1759. From a painting by Francis Hayman, in the W. Somerset Maugham Collection.

92. Scene from *Miss in Her Teens*, by David Garrick, Covent Garden, 1747, with (L. to R.): Elizabeth Hippisley (fl.1742–1768) as Biddy Bellair, Garrick as Fribble, Hannah Pritchard (1711–1768) as Mrs. Tag and Henry Woodward (1714–1777) as Captain Flash.

When young David Garrick left Lichfield to become a wine importer in London, the theatres were in the control of the Old School, with Quin, following in the tradition of Betterton, and Macklin as the principal actors. Garrick, attracted to the theatre made friends with Macklin and theatrical circles. His first writings were poems—followed by *Lethe*, produced at Drury Lane in 1740. He decided to give up business and try his luck as an actor. He made his first appearance in London at Goodman's Fields Theatre as Richard III in October 1741. This theatre in Whitechapel had opened in 1729, but lost its licence in 1737, when the monopoly of Drury Lane and Covent Garden was established. Giffard, the owner, evaded the laws for a while by various pretexts, including issuing tickets for a concert and producing a play free between its two halves. He

93. David Garrick as The Farmer, and Lucretia Bradshaw (d. 1755) as his wife, in Garrick's play, *The Farmer's Return from London*, Drury Lane, 1762.

Garrick had been with Giffard to Ipswich, acting under the name of Lyddal for a short time, before his London début, which took the town by storm. He acted many parts, including his own play *The Lying Valet*, at Goodman's Fields until May 1742. As he attracted audiences away from the Patent theatres, Giffard was again in trouble with the authorities and his theatre finally closed. Garrick was immediately engaged by Drury Lane, where he appeared in the parts he had played so successfully. A trip to Dublin with Peg Woffington followed.

94. David Garrick as Jaffier and Susannah Maria Cibber as Belvidera in *Venice Preserv'd*, Drury Lane, 1762. From a painting by Zoffany in the W. Somerset Maugham Collection.

returned to Drury Lane, remaining until 1745. He then went over to Covent Garden, returning to Drury Lane as partner with James Lacy in the management of the theatre in 1747.

He remained in control until he sold half of his share to Sheridan and his partners when he retired in 1776, retaining the other half until he died.

He married Eva Maria Violetti, a young dancer, in 1749.

His management at Drury Lane was one of the most successful in theatre history. Covent Garden tried to lure his audiences away with rival attractions, but Garrick remained the idol of the public. All the best actors and actresses of the day appeared on his stage. He produced Shakespeare (often in his own adaptations), revivals, many new plays of merit and pantomimes. His innovations and reforms, both before and behind the curtain, swept away customs that had lingered since the earlier days. His career is the history of the mid-eighteenth-century theatre.

95. William Burton (d. 1774) as Subtle, John Palmer (1744–1798) as Face and David Garrick as Abel Drugger in Ben Jonson's *The Alchymist*, Drury Lane, 1769.

96. David Garrick as Romeo and George Anne Bellamy (1727?–1788) as Juliet, Drury Lane, 1753. The scene between the lovers in the Tomb, introduced into the play by Otway and retained by Garrick in his version.

George Anne Bellamy made her début at Covent Garden in 1750. Her colourful career, on and off the stage, is told in her Memoirs, which she published in 1785. They also give an interesting account of theatrical life in the eighteenth century.

97. David Garrick as Macbeth and Hannah Pritchard as Lady Macbeth, Drury Lane, 1768. This performance (for which Shakespeare's text was used) was Mrs. Pritchard's farewell to the stage. She had established herself as an actress of the old school of Quin, before Garrick rose to fame, and became one of his leading ladies at Drury Lane. After their last performance together in *Macbeth* Garrick never played the part again.

She is reported, on being questioned about the plot of the end of *Macbeth*, to have said that she did not know, as she had never read the play further than the sleepwalking scene, and had always gone home after she had performed it.

98. David Garrick as King Lear, Drury Lane, 1760, with William Havard (1710–1778) as Edgar, and Astley Bransby (1720–1789) as Kent. Garrick first played Lear 1747 in Nahum Tate's version of Shakespeare's play, which he himself revised in 1756. It includes an extra heath scene for Cordelia (see Number 101), omits the Fool and has a prison scene for Lear and Cordelia in the latter part of the play. This adaptation, which ends without the death of Lear and with the marriage of Cordelia and Edgar, held the stage throughout the eighteenth century.

99. David Garrick as Sir John Brute in Vanbrugh's *The Provok'd Wife*, Drury Lane, 1763, with Henry Vaughan (1713–1779), Hullet, Thomas Clough (d. 1770), William Parsons (1736–1795), Thomas Phillips (d. 1768) and Watkins (fl. 1760–1772) in the character of the Watchman. The "drunken scene," in which Brute dresses in his wife's clothes and is arrested by the Watch is a famous moment in Restoration comedy. The part of Brute was known to actors as a "Drag Part," as was any female impersonation when long woman's clothes dragged upon the stage. This theatrical expression survived well into the twentieth century, still being used by older actors in reference to *Charley's Aunt*.

VICTORIA AND ALBERT MUSEUM

100. David Garrick as Don John in Fletcher's *The Chances*, Drury Lane, 1773, from a painting by Philip de Loutherbourg.

Garrick made his own adaptation of Fletcher's play and first played Don John in 1754. De Loutherbourg (1740–1812) was Scenic Director at Drury Lane from 1771 to 1779.

His innovations included the use of coloured silk screens pivoted in front of the lights to give changes. His cloud effects and fires were particularly successful. He was the first to break the artificial stage conventions and to introduce naturalness into scenery. He is credited with the introduction of the painted act-drop into this country. Many of his reforms were before their time, and his influence on scenic design lasted well into the nineteenth century. (See also Number 122.)

101. Susannah Maria Cibber as Cordelia in *King Lear*, Drury Lane, 1754.

The scene for Cordelia in the storm, where Edgar saves her from Edmund's ruffians, is one of Tate's interpolations in Shakespeare's play. The picture shows an example of the tragedienne's "Confidant"—always there to be addressed and to lend support, though she had no specified part in the play—literally a "supporting part."

When Mrs. Cibber acted Cordelia in 1754, Edgar was played by William Havard.

Mrs. Cibber, sister of Dr. Arne, the composer, and wife of Theophilus Cibber, first appeared in 1732 as a singer. In 1736 she became an actress at Drury Lane. She divided her career between there and Covent Garden, appearing in all the leading tragic roles opposite Garrick and other leading actors of the era.

102. David Garrick as Osman in Congreve's *Mourning Bride*, Drury Lane, 1750. Best remembered for its opening line: "Music hath charms to soothe the savage breast." The leading character only is dressed in appropriate Eastern costume.

103. David Garrick as Hamlet, Drury Lane, 1754. Actors dressed mainly in strictly contemporary clothes, with a few exceptions—royalty, cardinals and foreigners, and classical roles. Garrick gradually introduced more appropriate costumes for himself, though often the rest of the cast remained as before. He last played Hamlet in 1776.

104. David Garrick as Demetrius and George Anne Bellamy as Erixene in *The Brothers*, Drury Lane, 1753. The first performance of Edward Young's tragedy. It shows the typical classical costuming of the period, and the plumes always worn by the Leading Characters in Tragedy.

105. Garrick reciting the Ode in honour of Shakespeare at the Stratford-upon-Avon Jubilee which he organized in September, 1769. Though the first Stratford Festival, no plays by Shakespeare were included in the three-day entertainments of music and processions. The whole proceedings were unfortunately marred by rain.

106. Charles Macklin as Macbeth, Covent Garden, 1773. The first dressing of the part in Scottish costume.

107. Charles Macklin (1690 or 1697-1797), from an original pastel, in the *Picture Post Library*, made just before his retirement in 1789.

108. Charles Macklin as Sir Pertinax Macsycophant, in his own play *The Man of the World*, Covent Garden, 1781.

Macklin, thought by some to have been born in 1690, and others in 1697, had the longest career before the public of any actor, whether he died at the age of 100 or 107. He was last acting as Shylock in 1789—at either 92 or 99. He first appeared at Drury Lane in 1733. His epoch-making Shylock, which turned the character from the crude low comedian of the Restoration days into a dignified tragic character, was first seen at Drury Lane in 1741. He acted mostly in opposition to Garrick, and wrote a number of successful plays, including *Love à la Mode* (1759) and *The Man of the World* (1781).

109. *The Merchant of Venice*, Trial Scene, Covent Garden, 1767/68, with Macklin as Shylock, Maria Macklin, his daughter (1732?–1781), as Portia, and (L. to R.) Michael Dyer (d. 1774) as Gratiano, Matthew Clarke (d. 1786) as Antonio and Robert Bensley (1742–1817) as Bassanio. From a painting by Zoffany. Macklin attempted to play Shylock in 1789 but could not finish the performance.

110. Hannah Pritchard as Hermione in *The Winter's Tale*, Drury Lane, 1758, Garrick's adaptation of Shakespeare's play. Another version, *The Sheep-Shearing, or Florizel and Perdita*, was also in use at this period. It omitted the character of Hermione altogether.

111. William Powell (1735–1769) as Posthumus in *Cymbeline*, Drury Lane, 1764: Garrick's adaptation of Shakespeare's play. From a painting by Zoffany.

A pupil of Garrick and the first manager of the Theatre Royal, Bristol, in 1766.

112. Savigny as Oroonoko and Miss Miller as Imoinda in Southerne's play, Covent Garden, 1770. His first appearance on the stage. He soon faded from the public eye.

113. Anne Barry (1734–1801) as Sir Harry Wildair in Farquhar's *The Constant Couple*, Drury Lane, 1771. She acted also, first as Mrs. Dancer and lastly as Mrs. Crawford.

114. William Brereton (1751–1787) as Barnwell in George Lillo's *George Barnwell, or the London Merchant*, Drury Lane, 1776. A play first produced in 1731 at the same theatre.

115. Spranger Barry (1719–1777) as Romeo and Isabella Nossiter (1735–1759) as Juliet, Covent Garden, 1754.

116. Spranger Barry as Macbeth, Covent Garden, 1752, when he and Mrs. Cibber were rivalling Garrick and Mrs. Pritchard at Drury Lane.

Foote, first an unsuccessful actor, discovered a talent for mimicry which he put to good use at the Little Theatre, Haymarket, where he appeared in 1747, evading the licensing law by inviting his audience to take chocolate, their tickets admitting them to his entertainment. He wrote many satirical plays which were performed at his theatre, for which he obtained a Patent allowing him to open during the summer, when the other theatres closed. The theatre, partially rebuilt in 1767, was sold to Coleman in 1777.

117. Thomas Weston (1737–1776) as Dr. Last and Samuel Foote (1720–1777) as The President in *The Devil Upon Two Sticks*, Haymarket, 1768.

118. Riot at Covent Garden, February 24th, 1763.

The reforms of Garrick, which included the abolition of spectators on the stage, revisions of prices and methods of admission, had not been achieved without disturbances. The Georgian audiences, particularly the young bloods, were ever ready to cause a riot. One such, Fitzpatrick, had forced Garrick at Drury Lane to admit the public at the end of the third act at half price. He then turned his attention to Covent Garden, where John Beard had taken over management on the death of his father-in-law, Rich, in 1761. Beard refused to submit to the demands; whereupon Fitzpatrick staged a riot during a performance of Arne's opera *Artaxerxes*, causing much damage to the theatre. Beard immediately obtained legal protection.

119. John Beard addressing the audience, Covent Garden, March 3rd, 1763. The rioters changed their tactics, refraining from actual violence, but night after night so annoyed the audience with catcalls and disturbances that Beard was obliged to give up the contest and submit to their demands publicly from his own stage. The two broadsheets headed with these pictures, published at the time, give interesting details of the theatre at that date.

The struggle between management and audience was to reach its climax with the O.P. Riots of 1809.

120. Riot at Drury Lane, February 5th, 1776. Disturbances were not confined to differences over prices and unpopular plays, actors and playwrights also receiving similar treatment. At Drury Lane a farce, *The Blackamore Washed White*, by the Rev. Henry Bate, the unpopular editor of the *Morning Post*, was the cause of trouble. His enemies organized a riot at its fourth performance, and Garrick was forced to announce that the piece would not be repeated.

This satirical print is particularly interesting in showing the green baize curtain lowered, and the stage littered with the rioters' apples, oranges and cudgels. This riot occurred during Mrs. Siddons' first London season: she was, in fact, acting in this unfortunate play, and it had been Bate who had recommended her to Garrick for this engagement.

121. Sophia Baddeley (1745–1786) as Fanny Stirling, Thomas King (1730–1805) as Lord Ogleby, and Robert Baddeley (1733–1794) as Canton in Garrick and Coleman's *Clandestine Marriage*, Drury Lane, 1769.

King was a famous character actor, the first Sir Peter Teazle, Puff and Sir Anthony Absolute (see Nos. 145 and 147). Baddeley and his wife were highly esteemed in their day; he later was also in the first cast of *The School for Scandal*, as Moses (see No. 148), but is remembered today for his bequest to the Drury Lane Company of the annual Twelfth Night cake and punch, which is still served in memory of the actor who commenced his life as a pastrycook.

122. *A Christmas Tale*, Drury Lane, 1773. A dramatic entertainment by David Garrick. It was in this Christmas piece that De Loutherbourg's scenic experiments were first fully exploited. This picture is from a painting by De Loutherbourg himself. It shows Thomas Weston (1737–1776) as Tycho, and Samuel Champnes (d. 1803) as Nigromant.

123. Robert Bensley as Hubert, William Powell as King John, and Richard Smith (fl. 1753–1781) as the Messenger, in *King John*, Covent Garden, 1767.

124. Edward Shuter (1728–1776) as George Philpot, Henry Woodward as Wilding, and Michael Dyer (d. 1774) as Old Philpot, in Murphy's *The Citizen*, Covent Garden, 1766.

Arthur Murphy (1727–1805) wrote some twenty-three plays. Though not a good original dramatist, he was an expert in adapting the plays of others. His works paved the way to the revival of the Comedy of Manners. They include the comedies: *The Way to Keep Him* (1760), *All In the Wrong* (1761), *The Citizen* (1761) and the tragedy *The Grecian Daughter* (1772).

125. Samuel Reddish (1735–1785) as Posthumus in *Cymbeline*, Drury Lane, 1767. Reddish first appeared in London in 1767. He was a violent actor and ultimately became insane in 1779, and died in an asylum.

126. Francis Waldron (1744–1818) as Fabian, Elizabeth Younge (1740–1797) as Viola, James Dodd (1740?–1796) as Sir Andrew and James Love (1722–1774) as Sir Toby, in *Twelfth Night*, Drury Lane, 1772.

127. Mary Yates (1728–1787) as Electra, in Thomas Franklin's *Orestes*, Drury Lane, 1774. This actress followed Mrs. Cibber in the tragic roles.

128. The Entrance to Drury Lane Theatre. Designed by the Brothers Adam for Garrick, 1775.

129. "The overflowing of the Pit," Drury Lane, 1771, for a performance of *Much Ado About Nothing* with David Garrick.

The second Drury Lane theatre, built by Wren in 1674, though many times redecorated, remained much as it had been until Garrick commissioned the Brothers Adam to reconstruct it in 1775. Though it was again redecorated in 1783 by Thomas Greenwood, the old building was past repair and had to be closed in 1791 and pulled down the following year. Meantime the Company acted at the King's Theatre in the Haymarket (the Opera House), and later at the Little Theatre in the Haymarket, until the new Drury Lane was opened in 1794.

130. Interior of Drury Lane as it was when closed in 1791.

131. John Henderson (1747–1785) as Hamlet, Haymarket, 1777. He became established as the leading actor and successor to Garrick, who retired in 1776.

132. Thomas Grist (d. 1808) as Othello, Drury Lane, 1775. A comparatively unknown actor, but interesting pictorially to show the contemporary dressing of the part.

133. Elizabeth Hartley (1750–1824) as Cleopatra in Dryden's *All for Love*, Covent Garden, 1773, at which theatre she was a leading lady from 1772 till she retired in 1780.

John Henderson, after early struggles against extreme poverty, first appeared at the Haymarket in 1777 and seemed destined for a great career when he became the leading actor at Drury Lane the following year. He appeared in all the great roles: Shylock, Macbeth, Hamlet and Falstaff. He divided his time between there and Covent Garden, but died at the early age of thirty-nine, as a result of overwork and his early privations. He was buried in Westminster Abbey near David Garrick.

134. John Henderson as Macbeth, Drury Lane, 1778. The costume shows a return to conventional armour after Macklin's Scottish experiment in 1773.

135. Ann Pitt (1720–1799) as Lady Wishfort in *The Way of the World*, Covent Garden, 1776. Mrs. Pitt was on the stage for forty-four years and famous for her character roles.

136. Mary Robinson (1758–1800) as Amanda in Cibber's *Love's Last Shift*, Drury Lane, 1777. Famous as "Perdita" Robinson, mistress of the Prince Regent.

137. Frances Abington (1737–1815) as Charlotte in Isaac Bickerstaffe's *The Hypocrite*, Covent Garden, 1784. Acclaimed the greatest comedy actress of her time. Her career lasted forty-four years

138. John Moody (1727–1812) as Teague and William Parsons (1736–1795) as Obadiah in *The Committee*, Drury Lane, 1776. Two famous comedians of their period, in a play which held the stage from 1655 to 1788.

139. Jane Lessingham (1739–1783) as Mrs. Sullen and Charles Lee Lewis (1740–1803) as Archer in *The Beaux' Stratagem*, Covent Garden, 1775. Lewis created Young Marlowe in *She Stoops to Conquer* and Fag in *The Rivals*.

140. John Palmer (1744–1798) as Bajazet and Priscilla Hopkins (1758–1845) as Selina in Rowe's *Tamerlane*, Covent Garden, 1775. Palmer built the Royalty Theatre, Wellclose Square (1787), and Miss Hopkins married John Philip Kemble.

141. Oliver Goldsmith, dramatist (1728–1774).

Goldsmith is now remembered mainly for his play *She Stoops to Conquer* (1773), though he also wrote *The Good-Natured Man* (1768) and *The Grumbler* (1773). His novel *The Vicar of Wakefield* has found its way to the stage in several versions and forms: there have been over eight dramatisations from 1819 onwards, and at least two operas founded on the story.

She Stoops to Conquer marks a return to the Elizabethan style of Comedy, whereas Sheridan heads the movement back to the Restoration dramatists.

142. John Edwin (1749–1790) as Croaker in *The Good-Natured Man*, Haymarket, 1783. Edwin was a famous comedian, noted for his gagging propensities.

143. Edward Shuter as Mr. Hardcastle, Jane Green (1719–1791) as Mrs. Hardcastle and John Quick (1748–1831) as Tony Lumpkin in *She Stoops to Conquer*, Covent Garden, 1773.

Sheridan, the son of Thomas Sheridan the actor and manager of the Dublin theatre, was intended for the Law. He wrote his first play, *The Rivals*, in 1775, followed by *St. Patrick's Day, or The Scheming Lieutenant* (1775) and the comic opera, *The Duenna* (1775).

He bought half Garrick's share of Drury Lane in 1776 and became its manager. He adapted Vanbrugh's *The Relapse* as *A Trip to Scarborough* (1777), and wrote his masterpiece *The School for Scandal* the same year. This play, founded on the style of the Restoration playwrights without their licentiousness, marked a return to the Comedy of Manners and a new era in playwriting.

The Camp, a musical entertainment (1778), *The Critic* (1779) and *Pizarro* (1799), an adaptation of the German play of Kotzebue, with the pantomime *Robinson Crusoe* (1781) complete his works.

He was responsible for the rebuilding of Drury Lane theatre in 1794. After the fire of 1809, financial difficulties caused him to relinquish his management. He exploited to the full the popular taste for spectacle, and his productions were noted for their remarkable scenic effects and lavish costumes. He was also a Member of Parliament from 1780. His money problems and his multiple career caused his breakdown and death in 1816.

144. Richard Brinsley Sheridan (1751–1816), dramatist and manager of Drury Lane.

145. Thomas King as Puff in *The Critic*, Drury Lane, 1779.

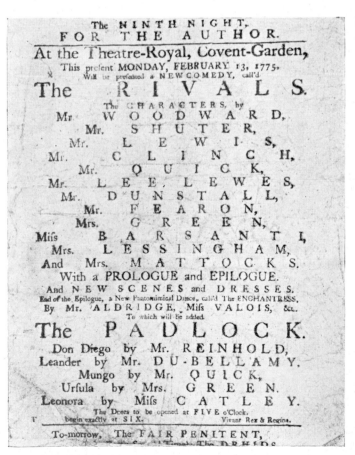

146. Playbill of *The Rivals*, Covent Garden, 1775. The ninth night, the Author's third Benefit.

147. *The School for Scandal*, Drury Lane, 1777. With Thomas King as Sir Peter Teazle, Frances Abington as Lady Teazle, William Smith (1730–1819) as Charles Surface, and John Palmer as Joseph Surface.

The Screen Scene in actual performance on the stage of Drury Lane Theatre, as re-modelled and decorated by the Brothers Adam in 1775. A fine example of the open wing and back-scene setting, then the usual method of presentation. Also the use of the fore stage, bringing the actors down to the pit audience, with the stage boxes behind them.

LADY LEVER GALLERY, PORT SUNLIGHT

148. Robert Baddeley as Moses in *The School for Scandal*, Drury Lane, 1777. From the painting by Zoffany.

149. A political caricature, 1789, at the time of the Regency crisis, suggesting that Sheridan did not wish the King to recover. It shows him peeping through the curtain at Drury Lane, attempting to stop the orchestra playing God Save the King. A point of interest is the footlights—wicks floating in tallow . . . the original "Floats."

150. Interior of the new Drury Lane Theatre opened March 12th, 1794, with a Concert of Sacred Music. Designed by Henry Holland, the entire building was never completed as planned.

This theatre, holding 3,611 people, was very much larger than the old house, which had lasted from 1674 and had finally to be closed in 1791: it held 2,000 people.

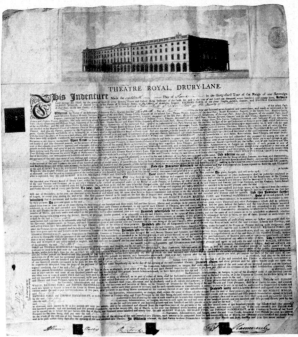

151. Indenture for a share in the proposed New Theatre. One of Sheridan's money-raising schemes, giving, for £300, free admission and half-a-crown a performance for a period of 103 years. From one of the original 300 shares issued, in the Authors' Collection.

152. Exterior of the New Theatre. It was surmounted by a tower on which was a statue of Apollo. The portion of the theatre uncompleted can be seen in the picture, when compared with the heading of the Indenture, which shows how it should have been finally completed.

153. Elizabeth Farren (1759–1829) speaking the Occasional Epilogue at the first dramatic performance in the New Theatre, April 21st, 1794. The play was *Macbeth*, with Kemble and Mrs. Siddons.

At the conclusion the audience were shown the new Iron Safety Curtain. Miss Farren informed them that they were now safe from fire. Tanks of water had also been provided on the roof, and when the iron curtain was raised the audience saw the water gushing down into a reservoir on the stage across which a boatman rowed. Notwithstanding this precaution the theatre was burnt down in 1809.

Dorothy Jordan made her London début at Drury Lane as Peggy in *The Country Girl*—Garrick's adaptation of Wycherley's *The Country Wife*—in 1785. She became famous in "Breeches" parts and such roles as Priscilla Tomboy in *The Romp*, Miss Hoyden and Lady Teazel. Her private life was as colourful as her stage career. She had four children by a Richard Ford before she became the mistress of the Duke of Clarence, by whom she had ten children. She last appeared in 1814 as Rosalind.

154. A scene from John Burgoyne's *Richard Coeur de Lion*, Drury Lane, 1786. With John Philip Kemble (1757–1823) as Richard and Dorothy Jordan (1761–1816) as Matilda.

155. Sarah Siddons (1755–1831) as Euphrasia in *The Grecian Daughter*, Drury Lane, 1782.

156. John Philip Kemble as Richard III, which he first acted at Drury Lane, 1783.

157. John Philip Kemble as King Lear, Drury Lane, 1783. In his first season he also played Shylock, Richard III, Hamlet and Sir Giles Overreach in *A New Way to Pay Old Debts*.

158. John Philip Kemble as Hamlet, Drury Lane, 1783. The first non-contemporary dressing of the part.

159. Sarah Siddons as Isabella and Henry Siddons (1774–1815) as her son. In Garrick's version of Southerne's *Isabella, or The Fatal Marriage*, Drury Lane, 1782.

Sarah Kemble, who had married William Siddons in 1773, made her first London appearance as Mrs. Siddons with Garrick at Drury Lane in 1775, but was not accounted a success and returned to the provinces, reappearing at Drury Lane in 1782 as Isabella in *The Grecian Daughter*, when she was acclaimed the best tragic actress of her day. Other members of the family soon followed her to London; her brothers John Philip (as Hamlet) in 1783, Stephen (as Othello) in 1783 and Charles (as Malcolm) in 1794. These with her other relatives and in-laws soon established the domination of the theatre by the Kemble family, which lasted for the next fifty years, despite the appearance on the stage of Kean and Macready.

160. Sarah Siddons as Jane Shore in Rowe's play, Drury Lane, 1791.

161. Sarah Siddons as Calista in Rowe's *Fair Penitent*, Drury Lane, 1782.

162. Sarah Siddons as Desdemona in *Othello*, Drury Lane, 1785.

163. Covent Garden Theatre, 1804. A Command Performance, in the presence of George III and the Royal Family, of *Pizarro*, Sheridan's adaptation of Kotzebue's play.

164. Dorothy Jordan as Cora in *Pizarro*, Drury Lane, 1799; from a painting by De Wilde.

165. John Philip Kemble as Rolla in *Pizarro*. He is also seen above (163). He created the part in 1799.

166. Stephen Kemble (1758–1822) as Falstaff in *Henry IV*, *Part* 1, Covent Garden, 1802. A fat actor—he played Falstaff without padding.

169. Sarah Siddons as Lady Randolph, with Mrs. Woods as Anna and Sutherland as Old Norval, in Home's *Douglas*, Theatre Royal, Edinburgh, 1784. This play, first produced in Edinburgh, 1756, and at Covent Garden the following year, was revived with Mrs. Siddons at Drury Lane, 1783.

167. Elizabeth Inchbald (1753–1821) as Lady Jane Grey in Rowe's play, Covent Garden, 1780. She was also a successful dramatist.

The Little Theatre in the Haymarket, built in 1720. Henry Fielding was manager from 1730 to 1737, when his political satires caused the introduction of censorship under the Lord Chamberlain and closed his theatre.

Samuel Foote followed in 1747, evading the laws until he gained a Royal Patent in 1766. He retired in 1771 and the theatre passed to George Coleman the Elder, whose son succeeded him in 1789. It was closed in 1820 and the present theatre built on the adjoining site.

168. William Farren (1754–1795) as Orestes in Ambrose Phillips' *The Distrest Mother*, Drury Lane, 1777. The first of his name and the founder of a long theatrical family.

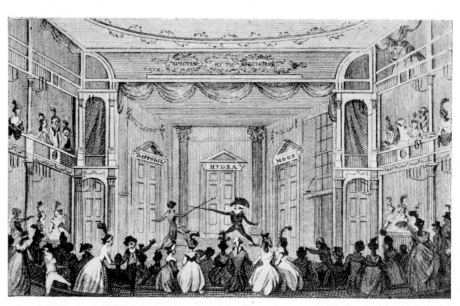

170. The Little Theatre, Haymarket, 1795, with a scene from Prince Hoare's *The Three and the Deuce*. This print suggests that an enclosed set was used earlier than is generally supposed (see number 241).

171. John Bannister (1760–1836) as Sylvester Daggerwood and Richard Suett (1755–1805) as Fustian in Coleman's *Sylvester Daggerwood*, Haymarket, 1796. From a painting by De Wilde in the W. Somerset Maugham Collection.

172. John Quick as Toby Allspice and John Fawcett (1768–1837) as Dashall in Thomas Morton's *The Way to Get Married*, Covent Garden, 1796. From a painting by De Wilde. Morton wrote numerous sentimental comedies popular in their day.

173. Charles Farley (1771–1859) as Francisco in Thomas Holcroft's *A Tale of Mystery*. From a painting by De Wilde in the W. Somerset Maugham Collection.

174. Richard Suett as Dicky Gossip in Hoare's *My Grandmother*, Haymarket, 1793. From a painting by De Wilde. Suett was also a famous Shakespearean clown.

175. The new Covent Garden Theatre, opened September 18th, 1809.

Covent Garden Theatre was burnt down on September 20th, 1808, and J. P. Kemble commenced to rebuild a magnificent new theatre from the designs of Robert Smirke. The new theatre, holding some 3,000 people, was opened on September 18th, 1809. Owing to the immense cost of the rebuilding (some £150,000), and the running expenses, which were estimated at £300 a night, as the theatre maintained four distinct companies for tragedy, comedy, opera and ballet, Kemble decided to raise the prices of admission.

He opened with *Macbeth*, and as he stepped on to the stage pandemonium broke out. Cries of "Old Prices!" filled the theatre. Thus began the famous O.P. Riots, which lasted for sixty-one nights; though the actors continued to play—George Frederick Cooke played Richard III in dumb show—not one word was heard above the noise of cat-calls, whistles, drums and rattles. Banners announcing the public's demands were displayed from all parts of the house. The police and soldiers were called and the Riot Act was read, to no avail. The whole town took sides and entered into the fray. Badges and medals bearing the words O.P.

176. The new Covent Garden Theatre, 1809.

177. Kemble as Macbeth during the O.P. Riots, 1809.

were worn by men and women alike. In the end, Kemble had to give way and restore the old prices, he made a formal public apology, and from the pit was hoisted a placard: "We are satisfied," and peace was restored.

In 1812 Mrs. Siddons made her farewell appearance as Lady Macbeth, though she was last seen as Lady Randolph in *Douglas* for the Benefit of her brother Charles in 1819. Kemble gave his farewell as Coriolanus in 1817 and retired, the management of the theatre passing to his brother Charles. The rest of its history belongs to later periods.

As a building, it was transformed into an opera house in 1847, and like its predecessor, burned to the ground nine years later. The present Opera House was opened in 1858.

178. *Henry VIII*. The Trial Scene, with Mrs. Siddons as Queen Katherine, John Philip Kemble as Wolsey, Stephen Kemble as Henry VIII, Charles Kemble as Cromwell (at table centre). Covent Garden, 1806.

This picture shows the principal members of the Kemble family. Mrs. Siddons was the eldest, followed by John Philip; Stephen was a year younger, and Charles the last but one. There were four other sisters: Frances, Jane, Elizabeth and Ann, and another brother, Henry, the youngest of the family, all of whom were on the stage. They were children of Roger Kemble (1721–1802) and his wife Sarah Ward.

179. John Philip Kemble as Cato in Addison's play, which he first acted at Drury Lane, 1784.

180. Sarah Siddons as Lady Macbeth, which she first acted at Drury Lane, 1785.

181. William Betty (1791–1874) as Young Norval in *Douglas*, Drury Lane, 1804. From a painting by Opie of "The Young Roscius."

182. George Frederick Cooke (1756–1812) as Richard III, Covent Garden, 1808.

183. Charles Kemble (1775–1854) as Romeo, Covent Garden, 1805. The youngest of the family, first appeared as Malcolm in *Macbeth* at Drury Lane on its re-opening night in 1794.

185. Mary Davenport (1765?–1843) as Dame Ashfield in Morton's *Speed the Plough*, Covent Garden, 1800. A famous character actress in the part made memorable by the constant references to her unseen friend Mrs. Grundy—who never appeared.

184. George Frederick Cooke as Iago in *Othello*, Covent Garden, 1800. Cooke made his first appearance in London in 1778, but returned to the Provinces. He reappeared at Covent Garden as Richard III in 1800. He remained there till he went to America in 1810, where he died two years later. His sensational career was marred by his incorrigible drunkenness.

186. Sadlers Wells Theatre, 1815, during the period it was famous for its Aquatic Dramas and Pantomines.

PART FOUR

Regency

(1811–1837)

HISTORICALLY, the Georgian era ends with the death of George IV in 1830, and the seven-year reign of William IV is but an epilogue before the drastic changes of the Victorian age. The years of Regency, from 1811 to 1820, have given a convenient and romantic name under which to group the artistic output of the early years of the new century. For once, the story of the stage does not fall so easily into the historical pattern. The true Georgian theatre passed with the destruction of Old Drury Lane in 1792; the following years are those of the biggest change, eventually leading up to the Theatres Act of 1843, when the Monopoly of Drury Lane and Covent Garden was finally broken, and the growth of Victorian Drama.

The Regency is a time of great actors and acting, rather than of drama and dramatists; though with the advent of Kean a death blow was struck at the "classic heroes" of the Kembles. The fashionable Georgian audiences had been driven to the Boxes; the Pit became the haunt of the middle-class tradesman, who wanted long programmes and spectacle for his money. Often the style of entertainment had completely estranged the intelligent playgoer from the theatre. In 1809 the O.P. Riots marked the triumph of Mob Rule in the theatre. Kemble had begun his reign in 1788: even before this he had brought forward his ideas on costume change. In France, Talma had begun to discard the conventional stage clothes and dress his classical characters in tunic and toga. It was on his lines that Kemble worked. He had big ideas and he began to stage his Shakespeare in a grand manner, to which the enlarged theatres gave full scope. In his twenty-nine years of management he staged eight of the Tragedies, all the Histories except *Richard II* and *Henry VI*, and eleven of the Comedies—which is five plays more than Garrick produced in his twenty-nine years at the Lane. In his work he was helped by the other members of his family, led by Mrs. Siddons. He realised the texts of Shakespeare were corrupt and began, as his biographer Boaden says: "to bend every nerve to make them perfect, beyond all previous example." He studied antiquities and costume in his aim to be exact. The result, to our eyes, is little better than the hash made of Shakespeare's plays by the Restoration playwrights, when the results he achieved are examined. He had good artists to assist him on the scenic side and his costume reforms were long overdue, but when it was suggested that he should adopt true historical costume for a production he retorted: "Why, if I did, Sir, they would call me an antiquary." It was left to his brother Charles, who succeeded him, to realise the project, but not until 1824, and open the way for Charkes Kean. But let all this not detract from Kemble's achievements. He kept the Drama alive against the odds of public apathy—a public which delighted in meaningless spectacle and the "Gothic" gloom of the German Romantic Movement represented by the plays of Kotzebuë. These were introduced to the London stage by Sheridan with Benjamin Thompson's adaptation of *The Stranger*, 1798, and his own version of *Pizarro*, 1799.

Matthew Lewis—better remembered as "Monk" Lewis, and for his *The Castle Spectre*, 1797—introduced into English drama, dungeons, ghosts, bandits and lurid gloom, which he allied to the spectacle demanded by the public. Much of this was to be incorporated into the newly evolved Melo-drama, of which the first example, to bear the label, was *A Tale of Mystery*, adapted from the French by Thomas Holcroft and produced at Covent Garden in 1802. In this new form, music underlined the action: Vice and Virtue are sharply defined in black and white: the Hero, the Villain, the Romantic Lover or the Distressed Maiden appear against a "penny-plain-two-pence-coloured" background, and a style of play was evolved which was to have far-reaching effects, and eventually to dominate the theatre for nearly a hundred years, despite the efforts of serious dramatists to break the spell.

Kemble—"the Last of the Romans"—retired in 1817: his noble, declamatory rhetoric had become outmoded overnight when Kean stepped on to the stage of Drury Lane in 1814. Time had come, as it always does every so often, for the appearance of what seems to each generation a "New Method." Macready had come to London and made his début at Covent Garden in 1816. Drury Lane was again rebuilt in 1812, under the régime of "amateurs"; the acting of Kean supported the House until control passed into the care of Elliston, "the Great Lessee," in 1819. Rivalry among actors again arose: Junius Brutus Booth was pitted against Kean: a contest took place between Kean and Charles Mayne Young—always leaving Kean the victor. Only Macready refused to enter into the conflict, not appearing with his rival until nearly the end of Kean's day. Elliston was succeeded by an American, Stephen Price, who brought Kean's son, Charles, to the stage; but Drury Lane could not find a permanent manager. Under Bunn, from 1834 to 1839, the theatre descended to the level of a fairground.

At Covent Garden, George Frederick Cooke had flashed across the horizon between 1800 and 1810. Eliza O'Neill had managed to draw away some of Kean's audiences from 1814. She was hailed as the successor to Mrs. Siddons, who had retired in 1812. Charles Kemble tried to keep the tradition of his family alive, but it was the Lane's turn to triumph—even Macready went over to the Lane in 1823. The fortunes of Covent Garden were not restored until, at the eleventh hour, Charles's daughter, Fanny Kemble, acted Juliet and brought a fortune to the depleted exchequers. Charles Kemble was able to retire from its management without debt in 1832. Charles Mayne Young, one of the remaining actors of the Kemble school, said farewell the same year.

On March 23rd, 1833, the theatre was the scene of the saddest of farewells, though not thought by the audience to be such an occasion. They had assembled to see Edmund Kean and his son Charles, as Othello and Iago, acting together in London for the first time.

The house was crammed to suffocation. Brandy had long since shattered the reputation, the genius and the health of the great actor. He had been very ill throughout the winter, and was utterly unfit to sustain the fatigue and excitement of such a night; but he went through the part, dying as he went, until he came to the "farewell," in which in the old days he used to stir the very souls of the spectators; he broke down on the words "Othello's occupation's gone!" Then, gasping for breath, he began, "Be sure thou prove—" but, unable to proceed, he fell upon his son's shoulder, moaning, "I am dying—speak to them for me." And so the curtain descended upon him for ever.

In 1833 the management of Covent Garden passed to Alfred Bunn, and he now controlled both houses for the next two years. He passed Covent Garden on to David Osbaldiston, a "Minor" theatre manager who tried in vain to attract the public by "reduced prices," though, it must be said, with a good company which included Macready, who had finally quarrelled with Bunn and left the Lane, and Helena Faucit, the last of the English Classical tragediennes. There seems to have arisen an utter indifference to the Drama. A contemporary describes the situation graphically:

"The drama, I fear, is in a bad way in London. Fashion is fatal to it. I meet young gentlemen who formerly used to think it almost a crime not to go to the theatre; but they now ask, 'Whereabouts is Covent Garden Theatre?' although the same people would faint away if it were thought they had not been to the Italian Opera. If they are asked whether they have seen Kean or not lately, they will say, 'Kean—Kean? No; where does he act? I have not been there these three years.' Formerly it was the fashion to go to the theatre, but now a lady cannot show her face at table the next day, and say she has been to the theatre. If they are asked whether they have been at Covent Garden or Drury Lane, they say, 'Oh dear no! I never go there, it is too low!' . . . I remember the time when it was no shame to go to see the legitimate drama."

In a final effort to restore the glory of the theatre and the drama, Macready assumed the management of Covent Garden in 1837. His struggle is part of the story of the Victorian era.

The first quarter of the century is rich in comedians, though their plays are mainly vehicles in which to display their talent. The names of Charles Mathews, John Liston, Joseph Munden, John Bannister and Edward Knight illuminate the theatrical scene, as do also the lighter actresses from Mrs. Jordan to Madame Vestris.

The rise of Vestris from a popular actress to be the first actress-manager—at the Olympic in 1831—and the scenic reforms she instituted there, are told elsewhere, and the continuation of her story belongs to the Victorian era.

As has been seen, there were other theatres in London besides the two Patent Houses in the eighteenth century: only the Haymarket had managed to legalise its position as a Summer theatre under Foote. The other outlying houses only had licences which did not allow them to stage plays. There is no law that cannot have a way found to circumvent it—and the granting of "Burletta" licences caused the growth of many small theatres in London in the early years of the century. This licence allowed spoken dialogue, provided it had accompanying music. Melo-drama was just the thing the managers were waiting for. Soon the Patent theatres objected, and it was laid down that at least five songs must be included in the piece to conform with the regulations.

This evasion caused the birth of a new form of entertainment called "Extravaganza" and later "Burlesque," which quickly became extremely popular, and even invaded the Patent theatres themselves; though the story of this side of the theatre belongs to the History of English Musical Entertainment from Ballad Opera in the eighteenth century to the "Revues" and Musical Comedies of today,

and is not part of our story here. They are, however, a very real factor in the cause of the decay of the Legitimate drama and its loss of audience.

This era also saw the rise of the outlying "Minor" theatres—often trying to circumvent the laws, and equally as often in trouble, but gaining the right to open when the Patent theatres were closed. As there had arisen a vast lower-class public calling for entertainment of the popular "blood and thunder" kind, the "Minors" gained strength at the expense of the Legitimate drama. To feed these theatres hack dramatists, often solely attached to one house, churned out melodramas, filching right and left from the French—and each other, there being little or no Copyright protection. In 1833 a Copyright Act was passed, giving some protection to dramatists, though it needed a second bill nine years later to reinforce this. Still, however, novelists could not protect their work from unauthorised dramatisation without resort to complicated means, until as late as 1911. The hundreds of "Minor" melodrama writers degraded the theatre and the actors' art, though some of the dramatists could, and did at times, write a play which had some merit and survived beyond its own day.

A new race of actors arose to interpret those plays; often they remained entirely in the "Minors," although sometimes reaching the West End. Some London actors could and did adapt themselves to the lower palate and serve both masters, but they were the exceptions rather than the rule. Edmund Kean played an engagement at the Coburg in 1831, when a local favourite acted Iago to his Othello. The audience gave their applause to their actor, causing Kean to tell them: "I have acted in every theatre in the United Kingdom of Great Britain and Ireland, and in the principal towns throughout the United States of America, but in my life I never acted to such a set of ignorant, unmitigated brutes as I now see before me."

The "Minor" theatres, however, were becoming a more and more powerful force in Theatreland. The Patent theatres—the last stronghold of the Legitimate Drama—could not make their chief asset pay; and as early as 1832 an attempt was made to abolish their Charter—a Bill passed the House of Commons but was thrown out by the Lords—but their days were numbered.

187. The Theatre Royal, Drury Lane, 1812.

 After Kemble left Drury Lane to go to Covent Garden in 1802, Sheridan was again in active control of the theatre until it was burnt down in 1809. This disaster made him a ruined man. He had no money for the rebuilding, but Samuel Whitbread, the brewer and one of the shareholders, raised £400,000. The Patent passed into the control of a committee with Samuel Arnold as Manager. The building, designed by Benjamin Wyatt, was opened on October 10th, 1812, with Robert Elliston as Hamlet. It is this building that still stands today, though the auditorium, as we know it, was constructed in 1921. The portico was added in 1820 and the colonnade in 1831.

 The early seasons were not successful. The theatre was not well patronised until the advent of Edmund Kean in 1814, though the Committee continued to mismanage affairs and lose money. They retired in 1819 and Elliston took control until 1826. After several short managements it passed to Alfred Bunn in 1834.

 In the new theatre, opened on October 10th with an Address spoken by Elliston and written by Lord Byron— a member of the Committee—proscenium doors were

188. Interior of Drury Lane, 1812.

abolished for the first time, but had to be put back by demand of the actors. The theatre was acoustically bad and alterations had to be made in 1814. The auditorium was still lit by candles, and the stage by lamps: gas was not installed until 1817. The auditorium remained lit during the performance. It is not until the days of Irving at the Lyceum that the custom of lowering the house lights came into being.

 The new company included Dowton, Elliston, Bannister, Mrs. Glover, Harriot Mellon and Fanny Kelly; but it was not as strong as that of Covent Garden, and though several newcomers were tried out in leading roles, it was not until the advent of Kean in 1814, engaged in sheer desperation, that the theatre achieved any success.

189. Joseph Munden (1758–1832) as Autolycus in *The Winter's Tale*, Covent Garden, 1807. A famous comedian whose career lasted from 1790 to 1824.

190. Eliza O'Neil (1791–1872) as Belvidera in *Venice Preserv'd*, Covent Garden, 1814. She was a rival attraction to Kean at Drury Lane, but retired in 1819.

191. Robert Coates (1772–1848). The eccentric amateur, congratulating Charles Matthews who had satirised him as Romeo. Covent Garden, 1813.

192. Harriot Mellon (1777–1837) as Mrs. Page in *The Merry Wives of Windsor*, Drury Lane, 1813. She acted there from 1797 to 1815.

193. John Pritt Harley (1790?–1858) as Sir Harry's Servant in Townley's *High Life Below Stairs*, Drury Lane, 1817. A play first produced in 1759.

194. The Olympic Theatre, Wych Street, Strand, 1818.

    The first theatre on the site was Astley's Middlesex Amphitheatre, opened in 1808 for equestrian performances, but proved unsuccessful. The name was changed to the Olympic Pavilion. It was taken by Elliston who renamed it Little Drury Lane in 1813, but the Patent theatres forced him to close. He managed to obtain a licence and re-opened as the Olympic, which he rebuilt in 1818. A year later he became manager of Drury Lane.

    Elliston made his London début in 1796 and soon became a popular favourite. He was ambitious to become a manager. He took the Surrey in 1809, followed by the Olympic, and moved to Drury Lane where he remained until 1826. His eccentricities and extravagances forced him to sell the Olympic in 1824. He was again at the Surrey from 1827 until his death.

    The Olympic remained an unsuccessful theatre until the management of Madame Vestris, 1831–1839.

    Minor theatres began to arise in Central London in the early part of the century, but, owing to the monopoly of the drama by the Patent theatres, were in constant trouble. Eventually they were granted Burletta licences, allowing plays, if they contained music and at least five songs, to be performed. The law was often broken, though the Patent theatres were ever watchful.

195. Robert William Elliston (1774–1831). From an original miniature, c.1807.

196. Edmund Kean (1789–1833) as Richard III, at Drury Lane, before the Duke of York, the Prince Regent and the Duke of Wellington.

Kean appeared as a child at Drury Lane in 1796 and continued to play in London until 1806, when he went into the provinces. He made a triumphant return as Shylock at Drury Lane in 1814. He introduced a new style of acting in opposition to the outmoded Kemble school . . . a natural style had triumphed over their noble declamatory methods. He quickly appeared in all the famous roles. Unfortunately his dissipations and eventually the scandals of his private life turned the public against him, though his genius continued to astonish them until his death. He was buried in the churchyard at Richmond, but his grave is now untraceable.

197. Edmund Kean as Shylock, Drury Lane, 1814.

198. Edmund Kean as Othello, Drury Lane, 1814.

199. Edmund Kean as Hamlet, Drury Lane, 1814. After his sensational début he was quickly seen in the usual leading roles.

200. Edmund Kean as Sir Giles Overreach in Massinger's *A New Way to Pay Old Debts*, Drury Lane, 1816.

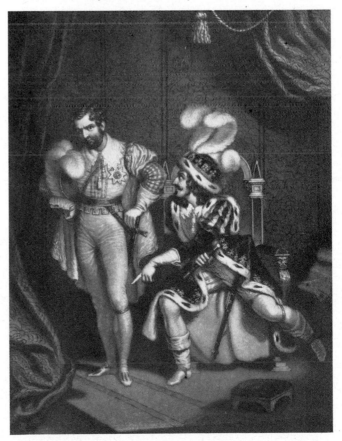

201. Edmund Kean as Lucius Junius in Howard Payne's *Brutus*, Drury Lane, 1818.

202. Edmund Kean as Richard III, with the Duke of Buckingham. This part became the most popular of all Kean's characters.

203. Junius Brutus Booth (1796–1852) as Posthumus in *Cymbeline*, Covent Garden, 1817.

204. Thomas Potter Cooke (1786–1864) as Roderick Dhu in Thomas Dibdin's *The Lady of the Lake*, Surrey Theatre, 1818.

205. Charles Mathews (1776–1835) as himself (r.) and as four of his Characters: Fond Barney, Mr. Wiggins, the Drunken Ostler and an Idiot.

Booth came to Covent Garden in 1817 as Richard III. He was immediately set up by the theatre as a rival to Kean at Drury Lane, playing the same parts. He accepted an engagement at The Lane, but found he was to play seconds to Kean, so returned to Covent Garden. Eventually in 1820 he did act with Kean as Iago and other parts, but the elder tragedian triumphed and Booth left for America, where he founded a famous stage family.

T. P. Cooke, a sailor before he became an actor in 1804, became famous in nautical melodrama "with Hornpipe," mainly at the minor theatres, until he retired in 1860. He was said in 1853 to have played Roderick Dhu 250 times and made 785 appearances as William in *Black Eyed Susan*.

Charles Mathews came to the Haymarket in 1803, after a provincial career. He soon established himself as a popular comedian. In 1818 he developed a form of one-man entertainment called an "At Home," which he gave at the Lyceum and Adelphi theatres, also in the provinces and America, combining these with his appearances in plays, until he died.

206. William Walborn (fl. 1817–1828) as Dusty Bob in T. W. Moncrieff's *Tom and Jerry*, Adelphi, 1821. The first play ever to be performed for 100 consecutive performances.

207. Frances Maria Kelly (1790–1882) as Brunette in Isaac Pocock's *Twenty Years Ago*, Lyceum, 1813. Fanny Kelly built the Royalty Theatre in 1840.

208. The Sans Pareil Theatre, c. 1816. Later renamed the Adelphi.

The Sans Pareil opened in the Strand in 1806 by John Scott, a colour maker, to exploit his daughter in her one-woman entertainments. He sold the theatre in 1819, and it was renamed The Adelphi. The theatre soon became the home of successful melodramas. It was enlarged in 1827, and Frederick Yates the owner —another one-man performer—was joined by Charles Mathews the following year, combining their work until Mathews died in 1835. Yates carried on until his death in 1842. The great days of the theatre belong to the régime of Céleste and Webster from 1844, when "Adelphi Drama" was established.

In 1782 Charles Dibdin built an amphitheatre called the Royal Circus, in St. George's Fields, in opposition to Astley's; this was burnt down in 1805 and rebuilt. In 1809 it was converted into a theatre by Elliston, who renamed it the Surrey the following year. He remained there until 1814. Thomas Dibdin (Charles's son) who had managed for Elliston, took control (1816 to 1823). Elliston returned in 1827 after his failure at Drury Lane. His finances were restored by the phenomenal success of *Black Eyed Susan* which ran for 150 nights.

209. The Surrey Theatre, as rebuilt in 1806.

On Elliston's death in 1831 Osbaldiston became manager. The theatre continued to present successful melodramas under various managements until 1849, when William Creswick and his partner Richard Shepherd made the theatre the southern rival to Sadlers Wells till 1869. It was rebuilt after a fire in 1865. From 1881 George Conquest from the Grecian—another minor theatre in North London—was manager till his death in 1901. From then, only spasmodic use was made of the theatre before its final demolition in 1937.

210. David Osbaldiston (1794–1850) as Hofer in Edward Fitzball's *Andreas Hofer, the Tell of the Tyrol*, Surrey, 1832. This playwright wrote a vast number of "blood and thunder" melodramas.

211. T. P. Cooke as William, Forster as Captain Crosstree and Miss J. Scott as Susan in Douglas Jerrold's *Black Eyed Susan*, Surrey, 1829. Jerrold was a prolific "Minor" theatre dramatist.

212. The Coburg Theatre, opened in 1818 under the management of William Barrymore and named in honour of Princess Charlotte and her husband Prince Leopold of Saxe-Coburg, became another Surrey-side theatre for sensational melodrama. In 1822 a large mirror curtain which reflected the audience, was installed. In 1833, as Princess Charlotte had died, it was renamed the Victoria and soon became known locally as "the Old Vic." The audiences were even rougher than its productions. In 1871 it became a music hall. In 1880 it was taken by Emma Cons and opened as the Royal Victoria Hall and Coffee Tavern. Gradually the concerts were supplemented with Opera and Shakespeare, under the régime of Lilian Baylis. The theatre was renovated in 1922 and again in 1950, after it had received severe damage in the Blitz.

213. The Looking-Glass Curtain at the Coburg, 1822.

214. The Coburg, 1818, with a scene from *Trial by Battle*, the opening play.

215. William Charles Macready (1793–1873) as Orestes in *The Distrest Mother*, Covent Garden, 1816; his first appearance in London. Although he appeared early in poor plays, he soon became established as a rival to Kean.

216. Edward Knight (1774–1826), the famous comedian, witnessing a performance at Drury Lane in 1825. He first appeared at the Lyceum in 1809 (Drury Lane Company). He excelled in "Rustic" characters.

217. Macready as Macbeth, Covent Garden, 1820. He remained there till 1823, going to Drury Lane until 1836. At first Kean refused to act with the new tragedian but eventually, during the 1832–33 season, he played ten performances of Othello to Macready's Iago.

218. William Oxberry (1784–1824) as Master Stephen in Garrick's version of Ben Jonson's *Every Man in His Humour*, Drury Lane, 1816. A mediocre actor of small parts at the London theatres, best remembered for his edition of plays and for his *Dramatic Biographies*, which were published by his wife after his death.

219. Tyrone Power (1797–1841) as Murtoch Delany in William Macready, Snr.'s *The Irishman in London*. Power became famous for his stage Irishmen from 1826. In 1840 he went to America for his third visit and was drowned on the return journey. His grandson, and namesake, followed his profession; also his great-grandson, the present Tyrone Power.

220. James Wallack (1795–1864) as Rugantino in M. G. Lewis's play, Drury Lane, 1820.
   Wallack divided his career between London and New York, where he and his brother Henry managed a theatre and founded a stage family.

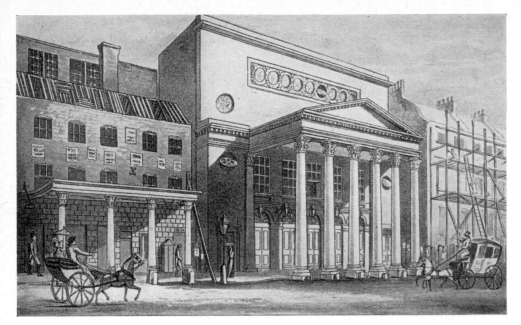

221. The Little Theatre, Haymarket, closed 1820, and the new theatre opened 1821.

George Colman the younger, who had succeeded his father as manager of the Little Theatre, had to surrender his control, through financial difficulties, to David Morris, his brother-in-law, who decided to rebuild the theatre in 1820. To conform with John Nash's London improvements, it was decided to build the new theatre on the adjoining site. Both old and new theatres existed side by side for a short time, until the old house was finally demolished after the new theatre had opened.

The new Theatre Royal, Haymarket, opened with a production of *The Rivals*. Daniel Terry spoke an Occasional Address, the entire strength of the Company appearing on the stage at the end of the performance. Thomas Dibdin became its manager in 1822, and many successful comedies were produced, including *Paul Pry* in 1825, when Madame Vestris sang "Cherry Ripe" for the first time. Dibdin quarrelled with Morris and left in 1826. Morris continued on his own until 1837, when Benjamin Webster, who had been in the Company since 1833, became the manager. Under the reign of the actor-playwright the theatre continued its success. He engaged Macready for the summer season with Helena Faucit as leading lady, and Samuel Phelps making his London début in the Company.

Webster remained until he joined Céleste at the Adelphi, of which he was lessee, in 1853. He was followed by John Baldwin Buckstone, who had been with Webster at the start of his management. Buckstone remained lessee until 1876—one of the most memorable managements in the history of the English stage. The plays Webster and Buckstone presented and the actors they engaged belong to the next era.

222. The Interior of the new Haymarket Theatre on the opening night, July 4th, 1821.

223. John Liston (1776–1846). The most famous comedian of his day from 1805 until he retired in 1837. Depicted as Paul Pry in John Poole's play, and:

(L. to R.). *Top*: Moll Flagon in Burgoyne's *Lord of the Manor*; Dominie Sampson in Daniel Terry's *Guy Mannering*; Lord Grizzle in Fielding's *Tom Thumb*; Maw-Worm in Bickerstaffe's *The Hypocrite*.

Bottom: Grojan in Caroline Boaden's *Quite Correct*; Lubin Log in James Kenney's *Love, Law and Physic*; Sam Swipes in Theodore Hook's *Exchange No Robbery* and Van Dunder in Poole's *'Twould Puzzle a Conjuror*.

224. William Blanchard (1769–1835) as Dr. Camphor; John Emery (1777–1822) as Andrew, Liston as Lubin Log and Charles Mathews as Flexible in *Love, Law and Physic*, Covent Garden, 1821.

225. Phyllis Glover as Eliza, Eliza Vestris as Phoebe, Williams as Colonel Hardy and Liston as Paul Pry, in *Paul Pry*, Haymarket, 1825. Williams replaced William Farren, who created the part, after a few performances.

226. Maria Foote (1798–1867) as Maria Darlington in Morton's *A Roland for an Oliver*, Covent Garden, 1819.

227. Eliza Chester (1799–18—?) as Beatrice in *Much Ado About Nothing*, Covent Garden, 1823.

VICTORIA AND ALBERT MUSEUM

228. Mary Glover (d. 1860) as Ophelia, and Charles Mayne Young as Hamlet, Covent Garden, 1826. From a painting by George Clint.

229. Eliza Vestris (1797–1856) as Mrs. Page in *The Merry Wives of Windsor*, Covent Garden, 1826. She also played Oberon in 1840.

230. Frances Kemble (1809–1893) as Juliet, Covent Garden, 1829.

Charles Kemble, who had taken over Covent Garden on his brother's retirement in 1817, had to contend with the popularity of Kean at Drury Lane, and try to find rival attractions. He produced *King John* in 1824 with historically accurate scenery and costumes designed by James Planché, the playwright and antiquarian. It was the first time an attempt at such realism had been made, and marks the beginning of a new epoch in stage design, eventually to reach its peak with Charles Kean, though at the time it was received with mild amusement.

The theatre did not prosper and by 1829 the bailiffs were in possession and it seemed as if the Reign of the Kembles was at an end; but the next generation stepped in and saved the situation. Charles's daughter Fanny, who had no wish to become an actress, was coached by him and his wife, who as Thérèse de Camp (1773–1838) had had a long and successful career. Fanny Kemble made a sensational début as Juliet, so great was her success in this and other parts that Kemble was able to pay off £13,000 of his debts in one season.

231. *Henry VIII*. The Trial Scene at Covent Garden, 1831, with Fanny Kemble as Queen Katherine, Charles Mayne Young as Wolsey and Charles Kemble as Henry VIII.

Fanny Kemble remained at Covent Garden for three years, bringing continued success to the theatre in the many famous parts, both in comedy and tragedy. She also created Julia in Sheridan Knowles' *The Hunchback*. In 1832 she toured America with her father. She left the stage in 1834 to marry and settle in Philadelphia. After her divorce in 1845 she gave dramatic readings in both countries from 1857 to 1868, when she finally retired.

Charles Mayne Young was a follower of the Kemble school. He first appeared in London at the Haymarket as Hamlet in 1807. He was a sound actor, overshadowed by his greater contemporaries with whom he played— John Philip Kemble, Mrs. Siddons, Kean, Macready and Eliza O'Neil. He gave his farewell performance as Hamlet at Covent Garden, 1832, when Macready acted the Ghost and Charles Mathews, Polonius—the part he had played with Young on his first appearance. He lived in retirement until he died in 1857.

232. Charles Kean (1811–1868) as Frederick in Eliza Inchbald's *Lover's Vows*, Drury Lane, 1827.

233. *Right*. William Grossmith (b. c. 1818) as Richard III, 1824. "The Young Reading Roscius." He came to London in 1827.

234. *Below*. Joseph Burke (b. 1818) as Hamlet. "The Irish Roscius" made his London début in 1825. He went to America in 1830.

Charles Kean, the son of Edmund, was not intended for the stage: it was to help his mother that he became an actor at Drury Lane in 1827. He played as Iago once with his father in London, on Kean's last appearance on the stage at Covent Garden in 1833.

Child prodigies had appeared from time to time in suitable parts, or in plays especially written for them. William Betty, the thirteen-year-old "Young Roscius," who took London by storm in 1804 in adult roles, was responsible for a new fashion. He played, among other parts, Hamlet, Selim in *Barbarossa*, Young Norval, Macbeth, before public opinion turned against him when he attempted Richard III in 1807. Retiring to go up to Cambridge he returned in 1811, but was not particularly successful, so left the stage in 1824, dying in obscurity in 1874.

Following in Betty's footsteps, child actors playing grown-up parts sprang up all over the country. Some achieved London, others reached only the minor theatres. William Grosssmith of Reading was in London in 1827; Master Burke from Dublin came to the Haymarket in 1825. He had his greatest successes at the minor theatres, where he played Romeo, Richard III, Shylock, Hamlet and Young Norval. He went to America in 1830, continuing his career in that country.

235. James Sheridan Knowles (1784–1862) as Walter in his own play *The Hunchback*, Covent Garden, 1832.

236. George Almar (1802–1854?) as Carnaby Cutpurse in his own play *The Cedar Chest*, Sadlers Wells, 1834; from a painting by R. W. Buss.

237. John Reeve (1799–1838) as Marmaduke Magog, and John Buckstone (1802–1879) as Jemmy Starling, in Buckstone's *Wreck Ashore*, Adelphi, 1830.

Sheridan Knowles, a mediocre actor, wrote many plays, successful in their day, including *Virginius*, which Macready created in 1820, *The Hunchback*, 1832 and *The Love Chase*, 1837.

George Almar, actor, dramatist and manager of Sadlers Wells, 1833–35, wrote over forty melodramas, all performed at the minor theatres. *The Cedar Chest* is remembered for the concluding masque, *The Silver Palace*, which achieved immortality through the Juvenile Drama.

Buckstone wrote over seventy dramas, farces and burlesques, while acting and managing at the Adelphi and the Haymarket. Though highly successful in their day, none achieved lasting fame; Reeve, a comedian in the style of Liston, whose parts he often played, had a short but brilliant career, mainly in the comedies and farces typical of his day.

238. Charles Kean as Hamlet, Covent Garden, 1833.

239. Ellen Tree (1805–1880) as Clemanthe in Thomas Talfourd's *Ion*, Covent Garden, 1836.

Charles Kean, after his early but unsuccessful start at Drury Lane, went into the provinces. He returned to London in 1828, achieving his first real success as Sir Edward Mortimer in Colman's *The Iron Chest*. From 1833 he worked hard perfecting his work in the provinces, returning again to Drury Lane where he played Hamlet in 1838 with great success. By this time he had begun to show his ability for archaeological correctness, which was finally to bring him fame at the Princess's.

He broke from the traditional Hamlet costume introduced by Kemble in a stage Elizabethan mode, devising a tunic which immediately became the accepted dressing of the part by other actors. The costume reached its final form in Kean's revival of 1850—and remained the stock costume for Hamlet until the 1920's.

In 1842 he married Ellen Tree, whom he had acted with on occasions since 1828. She had been on the stage since 1823 and had achieved a notable career of her own by the time of her marriage. She submerged her own individual ambitions to become his leading lady for the rest of their lives.

William Dowton made his first London appearance in 1795. He became successful in the old comedies, and as Shylock, Malvolio and Falstaff. In the latter part he made his début in New York in 1836. He took a farewell Benefit as Sir Robert Bramble in *The Poor Gentleman*, 1840.

240. William Dowton (1764–1851) as Falstaff with John Cooper (1790–1870) as Prince Hal and John Balls (1799–1844) as Poins in *Henry IV, Part 2*, Drury Lane, 1832. From a painting by George Clint.

241. Mathews and Vestris in Planché's *Court Favour*, Olympic, 1836.

242. Final scene from Mathews' *Why Did You Die?*, Olympic, 1837.

Vestris became the first actress-manager by taking the Olympic in 1831. Confined by a Burletta licence, she established herself with light comedies and extravaganzas devised for her by Planché. In 1838 she married Mathews, her leading man. Her main work was the reform of the staging of plays which till then had been acted before painted back flats and open wings with only the barest minimum of necessary furniture. She is credited as having introduced the box set in 1833. Certainly by 1836, in *Court Favour*, it had fully developed, complete with ceiling-piece in place of borders. Her interiors were fully furnished and appointed in the best taste of the period. Under Planché's influence, she also made period costumes more authentic.

She installed, in 1837, a fringed red velvet curtain, parting and drawing up from the centre, replacing the green baize drop which had been in general use since Restoration days.

In *Why Did You Die?*, the first play seen after its installation, the curtain was made an integral part of the plot at the end of the piece.

Vestris left the Olympic in 1839 to go with her husband into joint management at Covent Garden.

243. Charles James Mathews (1803–1878) as George Rattleton in his own play, *The Humpbacked Lover*, Olympic, 1835. He was the son of Charles Mathews.

244. The Green Room, Drury Lane, 1840.

PART FIVE

Victorian

(1837–1901)

WE enter the longest reign in English history on a note of deep theatrical gloom. Once again the historical divisions do not dovetail with theatre developments. It is not until 1865 that a new order of Victorian drama is born. The chain is then unbroken, though strengthened by powerful Scandinavian links, which are reinforced by native genius, until the contented era of Peace and Plenty vanished overnight in 1914.

On September 30th, 1837, Macready took over the management of Covent Garden with a revival of *The Winter's Tale*. Samuel Phelps, James Anderson and Helena Faucit were in his Company. Before Christmas came he had revived *Hamlet*, *Othello*, *Macbeth* and Lord Byron's *Werner* (which he had first produced in 1830), and numerous classic plays of the first order. In the month he lost £3,000. After the Pantomime season he continued adding many other famous plays to his repertoire, including *The Lady of Lyons*, a new play by Bulwer Lytton, which established itself as a financial success. He continued with a Company that was the pick of the profession, mounting his productions in the best possible manner, until July 1839, when he retired from the theatre a heavy loser. As we have seen, he had much to contend with in the debased public taste, even Queen Victoria herself visited Van Amburgh and his Lions three times in a month at Drury Lane in 1839.

His last production had been *The Tempest*, which was successful and for 55 nights averaged £230 a night. James Anderson says:—

"Had the manager only followed the advice of his officers, it might have gone one hundred nights more to like receipts. But no, he would never give the public what it wanted, but only what he liked; this he considered consistent with his pledges to give novelty and variety . . . Instead of running *The Tempest* nightly to fine houses, he chose to revive a dull old piece called *The Royal Oak* which he played to empty benches."

If Anderson is to be relied upon, even with public taste at a low ebb it could be drawn to the Legitimate Drama, and once again the words spoken by Garrick in his Prologue were proved only too true.

Macready was followed by Madame Vestris with her husband, Charles James Mathews, fresh from their successes at the Olympic. The largeness of the theatre defeated them though they had their successes, including

89

Boucicault's first play, *London Assurance*, in 1841. At the end of this season, £600 in debt for the rental, she was shut out from the theatre. Some short régimes followed, including another by Charles Kemble in 1842: the theatre then became the home of Jullien's Concerts and Bals Masqués. In 1847 its interior was completely transformed into an Opera House and lost for ever to the Drama.

Macready was at the Haymarket in 1840, where he had a big success with Lytton's *Money*. All his career he fostered the contemporary dramatist, producing four plays by Byron, plays by Browning and Sheridan Knowles; but his strength lay in the Classical repertoire. He returned to Drury Lane in 1841 as Manager, following his old policy, contending that long runs were death to art, and frittered away his financial successes. He indulged in productions of Opera and musical pieces like *King Arthur* and *Comus*; but the monopoly of the Patent theatres was nearing its close. The New Licensing Act was passed in 1843, mainly due to the exertions of Bulwer Lytton, and the Drama was at last free for all who wanted to perform it. Taste being what it was, there was not the expected rush to produce Shakespeare, and except for the rise to prominence of Samuel Phelps at Sadlers Wells little difference was felt from the new-found freedom. No new theatres were built, as had been foretold: it is much later in the Victorian era that the numerous theatres, many of which still exist, came into being.

Drury Lane continued to find little success with various actor-managers. It was the scene of Macready's Farewell in 1851. Seasons of Opera, melodramas, with occasional returns to Shakespeare or the classics, were its main fare till Augustus Harris became Lessee in 1879. His régime of Pantomime and Melodrama of a spectacular realistic kind, suited to the large theatre, became an established success until he died in 1896, and the same policy was followed by his successor Arthur Collins into the twentieth century. Here we leave the two great theatres, the real story of Victorian drama is carried on in the smaller theatres of the West End.

The Haymarket under the managements of Webster and Buckstone became established as a home for Comedy; the Adelphi became associated with Melodrama; Vestris and Mathews went to the Lyceum with Extravaganza and Melodrama as their chief attractions. Actor-managers arose, each known for a particular style of play or production, each establishing himself at his own theatre; playgoers knew what kind of entertainment they would see at any particular house. The evening's bill became longer and longer: often three or four different entertainments would be included—musical pieces, farces and ballets after dramas often made up an evening's playgoing. Half-prices after a certain hour still allowed a choice of fare. The prosperous middle class audiences filled the theatres; railways brought visitors to London; transport from the outlying suburbs, now fast growing,

allowed more freedom of movement. Fashionable Society was still aloof from the theatre, though the Puritanical "Victorians" often arose in their wrath through the mouth of the Clergy, using much the same words and arguments as Prynne and Collier had done in past generations. The theatre settled down to a period of solid prosperity, with plays of dull mediocrity. Playwrights from time to time attempted to keep alive the Poetic Drama, but Melodrama had a firm hold; its writing reached a high level of competence, though its general form remained unchanged.

Apart from Sadlers Wells and the work of Phelps, from 1844 to 1862, the main Classic repertory was in the hands of Charles Kean at the Princess's from 1850 to 1859. He went further than anyone had ever done before in lavish staging, with historical accuracy brought to the point of archaeology. Besides Shakespeare and other revivals he, like his fellow-managers, was forced to present Melodramas, mostly of French origin, which were more fitted to the tastes of the day. His nine years of management, though extremely well attended, could not, on his scale of expenditure, produce a profit, and he gave up before he was faced with financial ruin, to tour and make a personal fortune. Like Macready, he had kept the Drama alive and upheld the dignity of the theatre in the face of the lowered public taste.

It was not until 1865 that something entirely new came to the theatre: Marie Wilton took over a disreputable little theatre known familiarly as "The Dusthole," calling it the Prince of Wales's. Here she produced *Society*, by T. W. Robertson—and history was made. The plays which followed: *Ours, Caste, Play, School* and *M.P.*—were revolutionary, as was their presentation. Gone was the old style of setting and the mannered production: the plays were about real people and real situations, impeccably and naturally presented. The seeds of Madame Vestris's innovation of the '30's had come to full bloom and the theatre had become respectable once again. Fashionable Society took up playgoing: the day of the distinguished actor-manager had arrived.

Robertson was the first producer of plays as we understand it today. To him we owe much that is the Modern Theatre. His early death in 1871 brought the new trend to an abrupt close—the older dramatists could not or would not change; although a few benefited from his teaching, a new generation had to arise before his work could be faithfully carried on. The same year as *Caste* was produced, 1867, Ibsen wrote *Peer Gynt*—the way was opened for the "New Drama," but the theatre was not yet ready to receive it.

Caste was the first play to be sent "on tour" with a company completely reproducing the London production for provincial audiences. The provincial "strolling players" of early days had developed into the Companies which played regular Circuits, and from these grew the "Stock" system. Main provincial towns had had their own resident Stock Company, usually at a Theatre Royal—often enhanced by leading actors from London who travelled from town to town playing their famous parts with the local company well versed in the stock repertoire. This process needed little rehearsal: the main "business" of the play was traditionally stereotyped and the "star" actor or actress looked after himself, only giving a few necessary instructions to the company on his arrival.

The birth of the Touring system struck a death-blow at the old régime. Other plays and actors went on the road as a separate unit—sometimes with a repertoire of plays, or with a London success. Not until the rise of the Repertory system in the First World War did the provincial theatre become again, in part, a separate entity.

The theatre out of London rose to great popularity, the Industrial Revolution and its aftermath and the growth of quick communications all helping to this end. Many towns could support up to five theatres, with varying degrees of entertainment including the London successes, the plays suitable for the touring audiences only, musical pieces and later a Repertory theatre. It was many years before the Provincial pattern of theatre was destroyed by the Cinema and Television.

The return of fashionable Society to playgoing brought about changes in the seating of the theatres: gradually a few rows of stalls were created in front of the Pit, which had from the earliest times occupied the entire floor of the auditorium. In Georgian times the Upper Gallery had been for the uses of footmen and servants whose masters were occupying the boxes—the general public was mainly a pit audience. In 1880 the Bancrofts moved from the Prince of Wales's to the Haymarket, of which they reconstructed the interior. Mindful of the new audience they had created they abolished the pit entirely, replacing it by stalls, accommodating the old pit audience in an Upper Circle. The opening night witnessed a scene similar to the O.P. Riots of 1809. Bancroft faced their disapproval and stated his case, but remained unforgiven, though he won his point. Pits began to vanish further and further back, though the last vestige of the old stronghold of the playgoer did not finally disappear from London until after the Second World War. At Drury Lane it vanished as late as during the run of Oklahoma!: Gradually the upper rows of boxes had been swept away, making room for the Dress Circle and the Upper Circle, leaving only the few remaining side boxes as left to this day.

Bancroft also introduced a "Picture Frame" proscenium, complete on all four sides—a convention which, in part, still dominates the theatre. "Act drops" still remained in use, despite the innovation of a Curtain by Vestris. It is not till the turn of the century that painted "act drops" generally vanished; even then a few exceptions remained for many years. The playhouse had become established in the form we now know it, and the many new theatres which were to arise at the latter end of the Victorian era all followed this pattern. It is only in the new theatres of the 1930's that the gallery disappears, and at the present time the older theatres which remain are fast turning their galleries into either extensions of the Upper Circle, or re-seating them under the name of "Balconies"; thus making it possible for all seats to be bookable in advance—a final stroke to establish the respectability of the theatre. All this has been accomplished without any further riots or violent expressions of dissatisfaction. What remains of the old spirit of the disgruntled playgoers is now principally reserved for the occasions when a play fails to please.

After the rise of Robertson and the "Cup and Saucer" drama the theatre was not again shaken until the rise of Ibsen's influence and the coming of the "New Drama." The older actor-managers continued to produce the stilted melodramas in diverse forms: but gradually the new ideas began to be felt, though not without opposition from the older critics. Pinero, Henry Arthur Jones and their followers created a new Society problem drama, and Oscar Wilde re-created a Victorian Society "Comedy of Manners." The younger generation of actor-managers reaped a rich reward in the newer modes.

Unperturbed by all the trends from Robertson to Shaw, Henry Irving sailed a triumphant course at the Lyceum from 1871 to 1903. He followed the Macready and Charles Kean tradition of production with a classic repertoire and revivals of his predecessors' successes, adding little contemporary drama of real worth.

As is often the case in a period like this, the emphasis is on the actor and actress, and the Victorian times contain some of the most famous in theatre history. Irving, through his exertions at last achieved a social standing for the acting profession by his knighthood in 1895. Though still "Rogues and Vagabonds" to the Law, they could be "Ladies and Gentlemen" in the eyes of Society. The intellectual playgoer looked to the future and the "New Drama"—labelled by many as "nasty" and "shocking." Though, as we have seen, it influenced the Commercial theatre, in its own unadulterated form it only found a stage through the private playgoing Societies which sprang up in the '90's and were to be the main source and influence of new work for many years.

Through these Shaw first gained a hearing, and the type of play by which an audience was made to think, and not merely to be amused, grew up. Some of the Societies extended their activities into the Provinces, paving the way for the rise of the Repertory movement in the First World War.

As the twentieth century dawned the prosperous actor-managers and the insistent voice of the New Intellectual Drama occupied the attention of the two sections of the playgoing public. The echo of Nora's door-slam was reverberating down the corridors of the theatre.

245. Celine Céleste (1814–1882) as Madeline in William Bayle Bernard's *St. Mary's Eve*, Adelphi, 1837.

Born in Paris, Céleste went to America in 1827 as a dancer, coming to England in 1830. She first appeared in London at Drury Lane in the ballet *La Bayadère*. She acted mime parts in several plays at the Adelphi, 1832. She danced at Drury Lane and Covent Garden in 1833, returning to America until 1837. Her return to London marks the real beginning of her acting career. Her first speaking part was in *St. Mary's Eve*. After her fifth visit to America she assumed management of the Adelphi in 1844 (of which Benjamin Webster was the lessee). He joined her in management in 1853. She became directress of the Lyceum from 1859 to 1861. She made numerous farewells on both sides of the Atlantic between 1865 and 1874, only to return once for a Benefit at Drury Lane in 1878, in her most famous part of Miami in *Green Bushes*, which she had created in 1845.

She was the leading lady in her own theatres, and mostly associated with Webster in the typical spectacular melodramas which delighted mid-Victorian audiences.

246. Louisa Cranstoune Nisbett (1812–1858) as Philip, Duke of Aragon, in Aphra Behn's *The Young King*, Haymarket, 1837.

She made her first appearance when Miss Mordaunt at the Lyceum in 1825, but changed her name on her marriage in 1831. In 1834 she managed the Queen's Theatre, Tottenham Street (later, the Prince of Wales's). She was an actress in the style of Vestris—equally addicted to "breeches parts"—and excelled in the comedies typical of the period; her Helen in *The Hunchback* and Constance in *The Love Chase* being particularly admired. When Macready was at the Haymarket she appeared with him and created Lady Gay Spanker, in Dion Boucicault's first play *London Assurance* at Covent Garden in 1841. She had retired to become Lady Boothby before her early death at the age of forty-six.

247. Helena Faucit (1817–1898) as Pauline in *The Lady of Lyons*, Covent Garden, 1838.

Miss Faucit made her début as Julia in *The Hunchback*, at Covent Garden in 1836. So great was her success that she was immediately offered a three year engagement to play both tragic and comedy leads. Macready took over the management of Covent Garden in 1837 and she became his leading lady. During this period Bulwer Lytton's *Lady of Lyons* received its first production. When Macready left in 1839 and acted for a season at the Haymarket, Miss Faucit went with him. While there she appeared in the first production of Lytton's *Money*. When Macready resumed management at Drury Lane in 1841 she was still his leading lady, until he left in 1843. She continued to appear in London and the provinces until she retired in 1871, making only occasional appearances after at Benefits. In 1877 she laid the foundation stone of the First Shakespeare Memorial Theatre, where she played Beatrice two years later. A great actress of Shakespeare's heroines, she often aroused the jealousy of Macready.

Macready had risen to be the principal actor of his day, and though he presented the best plays in a grand manner, the tastes of the period were against him. His continued quarrels with Alfred Bunn, who owned both Drury Lane and Covent Garden at various periods, are famous. His seasons were artistically but not always financially successful. He tried to introduce new or unacted dramatists, producing the work of Byron, Lytton and Browning. He did much to clear the text of Shakespeare from the Restoration revisions. He took a farewell at Drury Lane and retired in 1851.

248. *The Lady of Lyons*, Act II, by Bulwer Lytton, Covent Garden, 1838.

249. Drury Lane Theatre during a performance of Macready's production of *As You Like It*, 1842.

250. Macready as King Lear and Helena Faucit as Cordelia, Covent Garden, 1838.

Considered one of Macready's greatest parts, which with Hamlet and Macbeth were universally acclaimed. He played an important part in the struggle to free the London stage from the monopoly of the Patent Theatres, finally broken in 1843.

251. Macready saying farewell at Drury Lane, February 26th, 1851.

He acted *Macbeth*, and during the "after piece" changed into evening dress for his farewell address.

Macready, who disliked his profession, wrote with satisfaction in his diary: "I shall never have to do this again—Thank God."

252. *The Chimes*, Adelphi, December 1844.
The first dramatisation by Mark Lemon and Gilbert Abbot A' Beckett. Another version, by Edward Stirling, quickly followed in January 1845, at the Lyceum.

The novels of Charles Dickens were immediately seized upon by dramatists and put on the stage, often before the issue of the book in its parts had been completed, writers inventing their own conclusions. Each minor theatre and some of the West End houses, had a dramatist on the spot to turn his hand to anything—there being no Copyright Law to protect dramatisations until 1911. Also the breaking of the monopoly in 1843 had made it possible for every theatre to act any plays they wished.

253. *Nicholas Nickleby*, Adelphi, 1838. A dramatisation by Edward Stirling.
Mary Keeley (1806–1899), who played Smike, with her husband Robert (1793–1869) managed the Lyceum from 1844 to 1847 and were a successful comedy partnership until his death, when she retired.

Dickens, though he loved the theatre and was himself an accomplished amateur actor, could never write a really successful work direct for the stage. He tried collaboration at various times with little success, with the possible exception of *No Thoroughfare*, written with Wilkie Collins, Adelphi, 1867.

Dickens mostly disliked the adaptation of his novels, and they caused him much annoyance. The only adapters who won his approval were Edward Stirling and Andrew Halliday.

From *Pickwick Papers*, written in 1836–37, which was first dramatised in 1837 before the completion of the book, until *The Mystery of Edwin Drood*, dramatised from the unfinished novel in 1871, the year after he died, nearly every story found its way to the stage in countless versions, often played at the same time at different theatres.

The only play founded on Dickens to have any lasting success was *The Only Way*, taken by Freeman Wills and Frederick Langbridge from *A Tale of Two Cities* in 1899, though this was mainly due to Martin Harvey's performance as Sydney Carton.

254. *The Cricket on the Hearth*, Lyceum, 1845.
The first dramatisation by Albert Smith, in which the Keeleys played, was followed eleven days later by Edward Stirling's version at the Adelphi. In 1846 there were at least nine adaptations, in and around London.

255. Samuel Phelps (1804–1878) as Macbeth, Sadlers Wells, 1847.
He restored Shakespeare's text, abolishing the Singing Witches and the music of Matthew Locke introduced by Davenant in 1672.

Phelps made his London début at the Haymarket in 1837 as Shylock with great success. Macready, fearing him as a rival, immediately engaged him for his Covent Garden company, keeping him under his eyes in secondary parts. He stayed mainly both at the Haymarket and Drury Lane until 1843, when the Patent Theatres' monopoly was finally broken.

He immediately took advantage of the new position and taking over Sadlers Wells, at first in partnership with Mrs. Warner and later on his own, he remained there until 1862. During this time he presented thirty-four of Shakespeare's plays—a record unbroken until 1923 by the Old Vic. He also revived many famous old plays and trained a generation of actors. His productions were of a high standard, avoiding the spectacular effects which were the hallmark of Charles Kean at the Princess's. He continued to act, after he left Sadlers Wells, until he died.

This was the greatest era of Sadlers Wells Theatre, as far as the drama was concerned. A theatre had been built there in 1765, in place of the earlier Music Room dating from 1683. It was to become famous for its pantomimes and water spectacles in the late eighteenth and early nineteenth centuries. After Phelps the theatre declined until rebuilt in 1930 by Lilian Baylis.

256. Sadlers Wells Theatre, Islington, 1850. This building was finally demolished in 1930, when the present theatre was erected.

257. William Creswick (1813–1888) as Hotspur in *Henry IV*, *Part* 1, Sadlers Wells, 1846.

    Creswick had a successful London career before managing the Surrey Theatre, 1849–1869, in partnership with Richard Shepherd.

258. Mary Warner (1804–1854) as Hermione in *The Winter's Tale*, Sadlers Wells, 1845.

    Co-manageress with Phelps from 1844 to 1846. Considered a Victorian successor to Mrs. Siddons.

259. Leigh Murray (1820–1870) as Orlando, and Fanny Stirling (1813–1895) as Rosalind in *As You Like It*, Sadlers Wells, 1847.

260. Isabella Glyn (1823–1889) as Cleopatra in *Antony and Cleopatra*, Sadlers Wells, 1849.

    Phelps' leading lady from 1848 to 1851.

261. Scene from George Macfarren's *My Old Woman*, at the Haymarket Theatre, 1845, with Fanny Fitzwilliam (1802–1854) as the Countess Xenia.

The construction of stages had undergone a change. Soon theatres too were enlarged and "modernized." Proscenium doors, abolished first at Drury Lane in 1812, but quickly restored, did not finally disappear generally until the end of the 1820's, though the fore-stages remained, not to vanish completely until 1880. Lamps which had superseded candles, gave way to gas in 1817, when it was first installed as stage lighting at Drury Lane. During the next ten years it became general. Electricity did not arrive on the stage until 1881 at the Savoy Theatre.

In an era of change, though Shakespeare and the drama were to grow more and more spectacular, an odd experiment, far in advance of its day, had been made at the Haymarket in 1844, when *The Taming of the Shrew* was staged in Elizabethan fashion by Buckstone. Though successful in spite of general misgivings, thirty-seven years were to pass before William Poel was to begin his similar experiments and lay the foundation of the modern staging of Shakespeare.

262. *The Taming of the Shrew*, The Induction; Haymarket, 1844.

263. J. B. Buckstone as Scrub in *The Beaux' Stratagem*, Haymarket, 1856.

264. The Lyceum Theatre as redecorated in 1847, with Vestris and Mathews in Planché's *The Pride of the Market*.

The Lyceum, originally a hall built in 1772, was rebuilt by Dr. Samuel Arnold as a theatre in 1794, but he could not obtain a licence. Various entertainments were seen until the theatre became the home of the burnt-out Drury Lane Company in 1809. It then obtained a licence, but only as an opera house. It was partially rebuilt in 1816, becoming the Theatre Royal, English Opera House, and was burnt down in 1830. The rebuilding of 1834 remained, with minor alterations and redecoration, until 1903, when it was entirely rebuilt, but for the portico which still stands. It was closed as a theatre in 1939.

The Adelphi Theatre came under the control of Céleste in 1844. Webster, who was lessee, remained at the Haymarket, running both theatres until he came over to the Adelphi in 1853. They remained there together until 1858, producing what became traditional "Adelphi dramas" as entertainment for the new middle class audiences. Webster's own plays and later those of Dion Boucicault were its greatest successes.

The theatre was rebuilt in 1858 and Webster retired in 1874; but the traditions were carried on by the Gatti Brothers with William Terriss as leading man. The theatre was again rebuilt in 1901. In 1930 it was yet again rebuilt as it now stands.

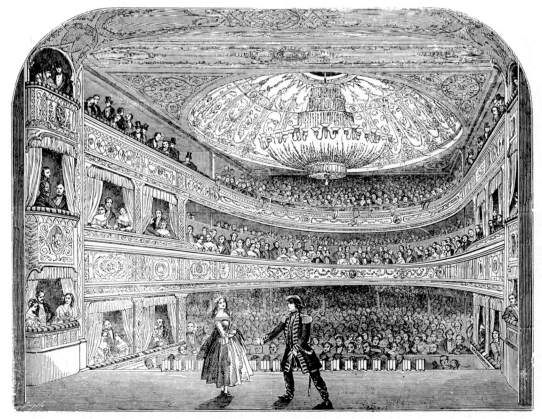

265. The Adelphi Theatre as reconstructed, 1848, with a scene from Samuel Lover's *Rory O'More*.

266. Gustavus Brooke (1818–1866) as Othello, and James Bennett (d. 1885) as Iago, Olympic, 1848.

267. Henry Compton (1805–1877) as Launce in *Two Gentlemen of Verona*, Olympic, 1849.

268. Kate Bateman (1843–1917) as Richmond, and Ellen Bateman (1845–1936) as Richard III, St. James's Theatre, 1851.

Brooke, a provincial actor of repute, fell foul of Macready and did not achieve London until 1848. Playing a season at the Olympic, opening as Othello, he was hailed as the successor to Edmund Kean. Like Kean, his intemperance proved his undoing.

Compton (whose real name was Mackenzie), a famous comedian in his day, was the first of the stage family. His son Edward married Virginia, youngest of the Bateman children. Their children are Fay, Viola, Ellen and Francis Compton, and Compton Mackenzie.

Ellen and Kate Bateman, the two eldest daughters of Hezekiah Bateman, an American actor and manager, were exploited as child prodigies by their father. Their younger sisters, Isabel and Virginia, followed in their footsteps.

269. *The Corsican Brothers*, Princess's, 1852.
The Vision scene in Boucicault's drama, with Charles Kean in the dual roles of Fabien and Louis dei Franchi.

The Princess's Theatre was opened in 1840 and used mainly for opera until it was taken by Charles Kean in 1850. From then until he left in 1859 he made it famous for the most spectacular and archaeologically correct productions ever staged. He not only produced Shakespeare and other classics, but English adaptations of French dramas. His productions reached a perfection which set a model followed by Irving and Tree, and which remained the accepted method for the next sixty years.

Shakespeare received severe cuts to accomplish the massive scene changes and to accommodate Kean's many interpolations. The immense cost of his productions could not be met by the receipts of so small a theatre, and this was his reason for leaving the Princess's, where he had "revived the Drama" and "rescued the dignity of the Stage."

His last years were spent in the provinces, Australia and America, with two London seasons—Drury Lane, 1861 and the Princess's, 1866, which made it possible for him to leave nearly £35,000 on his death.

270. *Macbeth*, The Banquet scene, Princess's, 1853.

271. Walter Lacy as Malvolio, Caroline Heath as Olivia and Ellen Chapman as Maria, in *Twelfth Night*.
 Kean first revived the play as his opening production in 1850.

272. Charles and Ellen Kean in *Macbeth*. Revived in 1858. Kean could never persuade his wife to sacrifice to his archaeological correctness her voluminous petticoats—a feature of the fashionable lady of the period.

273. Charles Kean as Leontes and Ellen Terry (1847–1928) as Mamillius in *The Winter's Tale*, Princess's, 1856.
 Ellen Terry's first appearance on the stage, Ellen Kean played Hermione.

274. Charles Kean as King Lear, Princess's, 1858.
 Cordelia was played by Kate Terry, and the Fool, cut in Tate's version and restored by Macready, was acted by Elizabeth Poole. Ellen Kean did not appear in this production, but in Australia in 1864 she played the Fool.

275. *Henry VIII*, The Masque, York Palace, Princess's, 1855. From a watercolour by F. Lloyds, one of the scenic artists at the theatre. The setting was designed by Thomas Grieve. Charles Kean played Wolsey and Mrs. Kean, Queen Katherine.

276. *A Midsummer Night's Dream*, Princess's, 1856. The Quarrel scene. From a watercolour by F. Lloyds.

In this production Ellen Terry played Puck, Fanny Ternan, Oberon and Carlotta Leclercq, Titania. The Keans did not appear.

Kean's principal designer was Thomas Grieve, and the original designs are preserved in the Victoria and Albert Museum, with a series of watercolours executed by the scenic artists engaged in the productions, made especially for Kean in 1859. These form a colourful and detailed picture of Kean's achievements.

277. *Richard II*, Princess's, 1857.

The entry of Bolingbroke into London—a great procession introduced by Kean into the play, in which between 500 and 600 supers took part, according to a contemporary report. The scene was considered even to surpass the glories of Wolsey's Banquet and Masque in *Henry VIII*, and to be the most spectacular of all Kean's efforts.

278. Charles Kean as Richard II, 1857.

The magnificent series of photographs which have survived of Charles Kean and his company from 1856 are the first authentic recording of stage costume at first hand.

279. Charles Kean as Shylock and Ellen Chapman as Jessica, 1858.

"Patty" Chapman was the Keans' niece and accompanied them on their long tour of Australia and America. Jessica was her first appearance on the stage.

280. *The Merchant of Venice*. The elopement of Jessica. Princess's, 1858.

Kean's claim to fame lies in his productions. As an actor he was never great: hampered by curious diction, he could never pronounce the letter N, sounding it as a D.

281. *Uncle Tom's Cabin*, Olympic, 1852.

Harriet Beecher Stowe's story quickly reached the stage as soon as it was published in this country. Over ten versions were to be seen in and around London between September and December 1852. The principal being at Drury Lane in December, it was by one of the most prolific of Victorian playwrights, Edward Fitzball, who was responsible for over 150 plays of all kinds and adaptations between 1817 and 1873.

The play became more firmly established in America than in this country.

282. *Philip of France and Marie de Méranie*, Olympic, 1850.

A play by John Westland Marston (1819–1890), who followed in the Bulwer Lytton and Sheridan Knowles outmoded tradition of pseudo-historical poetic drama. Though popular in their day, his twenty plays were soon forgotten.

Helena Faucit and G. V. Brooke were in *Philip of France*, the success of which, at the time, was said to have had an important influence on the fortunes of poetic drama.

283. *Ingomar*, Drury Lane, 1851.

A poetic drama by Maria Lacy (Mrs. Lovell), in which James Anderson and Charlotte Vanderhoff acted.

In the year of the Great Exhibition, London entertainments were mostly "popular," except for Kean at the Princess's. Anderson, a tragedian with a metropolitan and minor theatre reputation, took Drury Lane for a season with little success, though *Ingomar* remained a popular play for many years.

Charlotte Vanderhoff, the second generation of a stage family of the Kemble school; her father John being billed in the late 1850's in the provinces as "the last of the Kemble School."

284. Benjamin Webster as Triplet, and Fanny Stirling as Peg Woffington in Tom Taylor's and Charles Reade's *Masks and Faces*, a command performance at Windsor Castle, 1861. They created these parts on the first production of the play at the Haymarket in 1852.

Fanny Stirling had a long career from her first London appearance in 1836. Though going into semi-retirement to teach in the 1860's she made a triumphant return as an old lady.

Reade and Taylor, together and independently, were prolific writers of mid-Victorian dramas.

285. Alice Marriott as Hamlet.

A well-known minor theatre actress and manager. Played Hamlet between 1861 and 1865 at several theatres, and in New York, 1869.

Actresses as Hamlet have been numerous. The first was Mrs. Siddons (1777, in the provinces only). Jane Powell was the first in London (1796). The custom survived until 1938 (Esmé Beringer) in London and in 1957 (Siobhan McKenna) in New York.

Women also acted Falstaff (Julia Glover, 1833), Romeo (Charlotte Cushman, 1845), Shylock (Lucille La Verne, 1929).

286. Barry Sullivan (1824–1891) as Hamlet. His first London appearance, Haymarket, 1852.

He is best remembered as a provincial actor-manager, and one of the last to cling to Cibber's version of Richard III.

287. *An Unequal Match*, Haymarket, 1857. A comedy by Tom Taylor.

A writer of domestic drama and comedies from 1844 to 1878. His work preludes the coming of Tom Robertson and the "Cup and Saucer" drama of the '60's, after which some of Taylor's own plays develop in this form, though he returned to melodrama both modern and historical. Among his seventy-four works for the theatre are some of the most famous of Victorian successes.

288. *Janet Pride*, Adelphi, 1855. Madame Céleste in Dion Boucicault's drama.

Boucicault (1822–1890) made an early success with *London Assurance* in 1841. A prolific writer, he is credited with over 150 plays, many of them adaptations from the French, from 1838 until his death. He acted with his wife, Agnes Robertson (1833–1916) in many of his own plays on both sides of the Atlantic.

289. Benjamin Webster as Robert Landry in *The Dead Heart*, Adelphi, 1859.

Benjamin Nottingham Webster (1797–1882) came from a theatrical family and his descendants are still represented in the Profession by Margaret Webster. His career as an actor-manager and playwright is part of the history of the mid-nineteenth-century drama. As a character actor in his own line he was unsurpassed in his day.

290. Benjamin Webster as Richard Pride in *Janet Pride*, Adelphi, 1855.

291. *The Dead Heart*, Adelphi, 1859. By Watts Phillips, the most famous of his twenty-one dramas. This play of the French Revolution, similar in plot to Dickens's *Tale of Two Cities*, was revived by Irving at the Lyceum in 1889.

292. The Pavilion Theatre, Whitechapel, 1858.
The first theatre was opened in 1829, and burnt down in 1856. Two years later a new theatre was opened. It became known as "the Drury Lane of the East," rivalling its namesake in the production of spectacular melo-dramas. After many years of disuse it was finally demolished in the Blitz during the Second World War.

In 1800 only nine theatres were in regular use. Most of these were rebuilt or enlarged in the first quarter of the century. By 1850 over twenty-five theatres, some of which had only survived for a short time, had been built in and around London. The larger and better run of the minor theatres staged reproductions of West End successes, mostly in their own versions written by their resident dramatists, with their permanent stock companies, often reinforced with guest actors from the West End. These theatres flourished until the early days of the twentieth century and the arrival of the cinema.

293. The Marylebone Theatre, 1842.
A theatre in Church Street, Edgware Road, called the Royal Sussex, was opened in 1832. It soon became, in succession, the Pavilion, the Portman, and was rebuilt as the Marylebone in 1837. It had numerous rebuildings and new names: the Royal Alfred, 1866, and lastly the West London. It ended its days as a cinema, to be severely damaged in the 1941 blitz. The auditorium is now used as a store.

294. *The Colleen Bawn*, Adelphi, 1860. The Cave scene in Boucicault's drama, with Edmund Falconer and Agnes Robertson.

295. *The Octoroon*, Adelphi, 1861. The Slave Market in Boucicault's drama, with Agnes Robertson, Samuel Emery and Dion Boucicault.

296. *It's Never Too Late to Mend*, Princess's, 1865. The Australian Goldfields scene in Charles Reade's adaptation of his own novel.

Among Boucicault's many plays the most famous are the American and Irish dramas. *The Colleen Bawn*, was still being acted in the 1920's. His plays, *The Shaughrann* (1875), *The Streets of London* (1864), have both been revived in recent years, proving themselves to be among the best written and constructed plays of their era.

Charles Reade, principally a novelist, though he longed for success in the theatre, achieved this mostly in collaborations. *The Courier of Lyons (The Lyons Mail)*, an adaptation from the French, Princess's, 1854, provided a famous dual role for Charles Kean, the Irvings and Martin Harvey. *It's Never Too Late to Mend*, caused a first night sensation. Members of the audience protested at the all too realistic Treadmill scene in this drama of "modern social life."

297. Kate Saville as May Edwards, singing "The Maniac's Dream," in Tom Taylor's *The Ticket-of-Leave Man*, Olympic, 1863. This most famous melodrama, constantly revived into the early twentieth century and seen again at the Arts Theatre, 1956.

Incidental songs were often introduced into melodramas as part of the plot.

298. Kate Terry (1844–1924) and Henry Neville (1837–1910) in *The Serf, or Love Levels All*, Olympic, 1865.

Henry Neville, the hero of many melodramas at the Olympic, was a flamboyant and romantic actor typical of the mid-Victorian school. He acted in the Drury Lane melodramas from 1885 until his death.

299. Charles Fechter (1824–1879) as Hamlet, Princess's, 1861.

An Anglo-French actor who appeared in Europe and America with equal success. His Hamlet was revolutionary. He abandoned old traditions, played the part in a flaxen wig, and made many innovations, which became accepted.

300. *The Ticket-of-Leave Man*, Olympic, 1863. The Office scene, with Henry Neville (R.) as Bob Brierley.

301. Edward Sothern (1826–1881) as Lord Dundreary in *Our American Cousin*. First produced in America, 1858, and at the Haymarket, 1861. It was constantly revived until 1879.

Dundreary was originally a subsidiary part in Tom Taylor's play, considerably built up by the actor himself into one of the most famous eccentric comedy figures of the day.

302. Jane Woolgar and Benjamin Webster in Charles Dickens' and Wilkie Collins' *No Thoroughfare*, Adelphi, 1867.

The most successful of Dickens' direct associations with the theatre. Collins, remembered as a novelist, wrote fourteen plays between 1857 and 1885, which include versions of his own stories.

303. Kate Bateman as Leah in *Leah, the Forsaken*, Adelphi, 1863. Her reappearance as an actress, in a drama by Augustin Daly, the American producer and manager, who also wrote twenty miscellaneous plays, most of which received their first production in America. He built Daly's Theatre, London, in 1893.

304. E. A. Sothern and Kate Saville in Westland Marston's *The Favourite of Fortune*, Haymarket, 1866.

305. George Honey (1822–1880) as Eccles in *Caste*, Prince of Wales's, 1867.

306. John Hare (1844–1921) as Sam Gerridge, and Marie Wilton (1838–1921) as Polly Eccles in *Caste*, 1867.

307. Squire Bancroft (1841–1926) as Captain Hawtree in *Caste*, 1867.

Marie Wilton, a burlesque actress, went into management, 1865, taking the theatre in Tottenham Street which had been opening under various names since the late eighteenth century. She refurbished and rechristened it The Prince of Wales's. Here began modern comedy staging and production as we understand it today. With Bancroft as her leading man, whom she married in 1867, and the plays of T. W. Robertson (1829–1871), she brought Society back to the theatre, making playgoing again a fashionable pursuit. The "Cup and Saucer" plays of Robertson commenced with *Society*, 1865, followed yearly by *Ours*, *Caste*, *Play*, *School* and *M.P.*

308. *Ours*, Prince of Wales's, 1866. The Crimean Hut scene, designed by Charles S. James.

309. Mr. and Mrs. Kendal as Dora and Julian in *Diplomacy*, Prince of Wales's, 1878.

310. Mrs. Bancroft as Countess Zicka in *Diplomacy*, 1878. The play was adapted from Sardou's *Dora* by Clement Scott and B. C. Stephenson.

311. John Hare as Lord Killclare in Charles Coghlan's *A Quiet Rubber*, Court, 1876.

After Robertson's early death the Bancrofts were forced to return to "adaptations from the French" which he had tried to supersede. Unfortunately the contemporary melodrama-bred dramatists could not adapt themselves to his more natural and refined style; though his influence was felt, nearly twenty years were to pass and a new generation of writers arise before his work was carried on.

The Bancrofts continued at the Prince of Wales's until 1880, moving to the Haymarket. John Hare, a brilliant character actor, went into management at the Court Theatre in 1875.

312. The cast of H. J. Byron's *Our Boys*, Vaudeville, 1875. This was the first play to run for 500 successive performances on its first production.

The Terry sisters, Kate, Ellen and Marion, with their brothers Fred and Charles, were the second generation of the greatest of English stage families. Kate became the mother of Mabel Terry-Lewis and Kate Terry-Lewis, who is the mother of John Gielgud. With other members of the family, their in-laws and descendants, their influence is spread over the theatre in all its branches.

Edith and Gordon Craig, the children of Ellen Terry, made their first stage appearance in *Olivia*.

313. The cast of W. G. Wills' *Olivia*, Court Theatre, 1878. Ellen Terry, centre, resting on Herman Vezin's knee. The children are Edith and Gordon Craig.

314. Madge Robertson (1848–1935) and William Kendal (1843–1917) in W. S. Gilbert's *Pygmalion and Galatea*, Haymarket, 1871.

The Kendals, married in 1869, were with the Bancrofts, and later with Hare at the Court, joining him in management of the St. James's, 1878–1888.

315. Marion Terry (1852–1930) as Dorothy in W. S. Gilbert's drama *Dan'l Druce, Blacksmith*, Haymarket, 1876.

Gilbert's early comedies were extremely successful, more so than his dramas, but his playwriting is overshadowed by his association with Arthur Sullivan.

316. Julia Stewart and George Honey in *Engaged*, Haymarket, 1877, a farcical comedy by W. S. Gilbert (1836–1911).

He experimented with many styles of playwriting: Burlesques, Farces, Extravaganzas and Dramas, and wrote some fifty pieces apart from his Comic Operas with Arthur Sullivan.

317. Herman Vezin (1829–1910) as Pierre Lorance in F. C. Burnand's *Proof*, Adelphi, 1878.
Vezin, a fine classical actor, was overshadowed by Irving.

318. Charles Warner (1848–1909), as Coupeau in *Drink*, Princess's, 1879. Charles Reade's adaptation of Zola's *L'Assommoir*: a melodramatic actor in his most famous part.

319. Clara Dowse (Mrs. Rousby) (1852–1879) as Joan of Arc, Queen's, 1871. A favourite costume actress in Tom Taylor's historical drama, at the Queen's Theatre, Long Acre, which flourished from 1867 to 1878. The site is now covered by Odham's Press.

320. Jenny Lee (1859–1930) as Jo in the title role of J. P. Burnett's version of Dickens' *Bleak House*, Globe, 1876.

A part she played several thousand times all over the world until the end of the century.

321. Ada Cavendish (1847–1895), as Mercy Merrick in Wilkie Collins' *The New Magdalen*, Olympic, 1873.

An actress manager of both the Olympic and St. James's, among other theatres, in her most famous role, in which she also appeared in America.

322. Adelaide Neilson (1848–1880) as Juliet, Haymarket, 1876. From 1865, she was a favourite exponent of Shakespeare's heroines, both here and in America; Juliet being her most famous part.

323. Isabel Bateman (1854–1934) as Fanchette in W. G. Wills' play, Lyceum, 1871. Her grown-up début. She retired in 1898 to enter a convent.

324. Geneviève Ward (1838–1922) as Stéphanie in Herman Merivale's and F. C. Grove's *Forget-Me-Not*, Lyceum, 1879. A Shakespearean "heavy woman," acted with Irving and Benson. Last appeared as Volumnia at the Old Vic in 1920.

325. Henry Irving as Charles I, the title role of W. G. Wills' play, Lyceum, 1872.

326. Irving as Mathias in Leopold Lewis' *The Bells*, Lyceum, 1871.

327. Irving as Shylock, Lyceum, 1879. His first revival of *The Merchant of Venice*.

Henry Irving (1838–1905) made his début at Sunderland in 1856. He came to London in 1859 as Johnson in John Oxenford's *Ivy Hall* at the Princess's. Other engagements followed in the provinces and London after a successful return in 1866. He was engaged in 1871 as leading man by Bateman, who had taken the Lyceum to exploit his daughters as grown-up actresses. The management was not successful, and Irving persuaded Bateman to let him produce a play he had found called *The Bells*. In desperation Bateman agreed.

328. Irving as Hamlet, Lyceum, 1874.
His performance was acclaimed the ideal interpretation. Running for 200 performances it created a record still unsurpassed. It was revived to inaugurate his own management in 1878.

329. Irving as Dr. Primrose and Ellen Terry in *Olivia*, Lyceum, 1885. Ellen Terry joined Irving in 1878, to play Ophelia, and remained with him until 1902.

330. Irving as Macbeth, Lyceum, 1875.
He was never photographed in plays between 1880 and 1890, except for the series in *Olivia*—his only ones with Ellen Terry.

331. Ellen Terry and Gordon Craig in Charles Reade's *Nance Oldfield*, Lyceum, 1891.

332. Irving as Mephistopheles in W. G. Wills' version of Goethe's *Faust*, Lyceum, 1885.

333. Ellen Terry as Beatrice, in *Much Ado About Nothing*, Lyceum, 1882.

Irving created an overnight sensation as Mathias. He followed this with a number of revivals of well-known plays and new plays especially written for him, including *Charles I*, 1872, *Philip*, 1874. His first Shakespearean production at the Lyceum was *Hamlet*, followed by *Macbeth* and *Othello*; in 1876 Tennyson's *Queen Mary* was produced, and in 1877, *Richard III*.

Irving had a love of the old dramas made famous by Macready and Charles Kean. He revived Lytton's *Richelieu* in 1873, *The Lyons Mail* in 1877 and Boucicault's *Louis XI* in 1878. One of his early innovations was the lowering of the auditorium lights during the action of play, though at what precise date this occurred appears to be unrecorded.

334. Irving and the Lyceum Company in Laurence Irving's translation of Sardou's *Robespierre*, first produced at the Lyceum, 1899.

Irving's aversion to the camera prevented any stage scenes of his productions being photographed at the Lyceum, even when this became possible in the mid '90's. This unique example was taken in New York during an American tour following the London production.

335. Irving as Becket, the title role of Alfred Tennyson's play, Lyceum, 1893.

It was the last part he acted before his death at Bradford while on tour in 1905. He was buried in Westminster Abbey.

336. *Macbeth*: The Sleep-walking scene, Lyceum, 1888.

In December 1878 Irving assumed full management of the Lyceum and engaged Ellen Terry as his leading lady. They remained together from then until he left the theatre in 1903. His career was marked by a triumphant series of revivals of Shakespeare and other plays. Unfortunately Irving mainly relied on earlier and tried successes which were old-fashioned even in his day—only his genius could make them acceptable. His new plays were mainly written in an older style by dramatists of little worth, though he did manage to bring to the theatre the almost unactable plays of Tennyson.

He presented costume drama with one dismal exception, *The Medicine Man* (1898), in which the sight of Irving in a frock coat was completely unacceptable.

Irving refused to move with the times. Electricity was not allowed on the stage of the theatre for his productions. The "New Drama" was not for him, and he became outmoded before his time, though he did more than any other actor to raise the status of his profession from the traditional "Rogues and Vagabonds" to the rank of Ladies and Gentlemen. His knighthood in 1895 marked the peak of his career. From then on the stage was recognized as a respectable occupation.

David Garrick had hoped and expected to be knighted on his retirement, but the theatre had to wait for this distinction until Irving. From then, the stage has been regularly honoured in all its branches.

337. *Henry VIII*, The Masque scene, Lyceum, 1892.

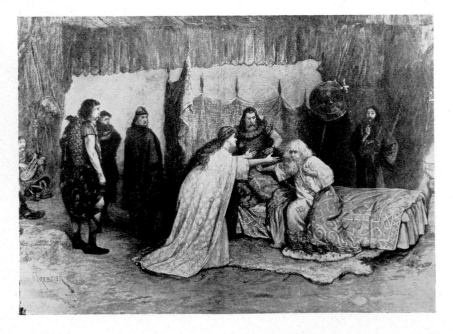

The second half of the century saw the building of many new theatres. This had been expected after the Theatre Act of 1843, but was not so soon coming as had been thought.

Between 1860 and 1870 five new theatres were opened; another five between 1870–80; ten between 1880–90, and another four by the end of the century. Some were soon to be swept away by the London improvements of the '90's, but the majority remained in use. No new wave of theatre building occurred until the 1930's. Today we are left with what still remains of the Victorian and Edwardian theatres and the contrasting newer buildings, making a conflicting mixture of styles.

338. *King Lear*, Lyceum, 1892.
Irving as Lear and Ellen **Terry** as Cordelia.

339. Herbert Beerbohm Tree (1853–1917) as the Rev. Robert Spalding in Charles Hawtrey's *The Private Secretary*, Prince's (later Prince of Wales's) 1884.

The part was later to become associated with W. S. Penley.

340. John Laurence Toole (1830–1906) and Eliza Johnstone in *Dot*, Boucicault's adaptation of Dickens' *The Cricket on the Hearth*, Folly Theatre, 1880.

Toole first played Caleb Plummer in 1862.

341. Arthur Cecil as Mr. Posket in *The Magistrate*, Court, 1885.

One of the famous early farces by Arthur Pinero, written before he became a Society-Problem dramatist. Others include, *The Schoolmistress*, 1886 and *Dandy Dick*, 1887.

342. *The Balloon*, Strand Theatre, 1889. A farcical comedy by J. H. Darnley and G. Melville Fenn, with George Giddens and Ellaline Terriss (centre).

The Strand Theatre originally opened in 1820, became famous as a burlesque house from 1858 to 1872. Rebuilt in 1882, it became the home of successful farces until pulled down in 1905. On the site is now Aldwych Tube Station.

343. Charles Collette and Minnie Terry in Hugh Moss's *Bootle's Baby*, Globe, 1888. The début of Minnie Terry, daughter of Charles Terry.

The Globe Theatre, Newcastle Street, Strand, was opened in 1868 and was in use until 1902, but it was never a highly successful house.

344. *The Lights o' London*, The Regent's Canal scene, Princess's, 1881, a melodrama by George R. Sims.

After Charles Kean's day this theatre became another melodrama house, memorable mainly for the management of Wilson Barrett, 1881 to 1886, during which he produced *The Silver King*. The theatre was closed in 1902 and used as a warehouse until it was finally demolished in 1931.

345. Jessie Milward and William Terriss in *The Harbour Lights*, Adelphi, 1885, by George R. Sims and Henry Pettitt, who wrote numerous melodramas.

Terriss, a leading actor with Irving, was also the hero of many Adelphi dramas. He was assassinated by a madman while entering the theatre in 1897.

346. Scenes from *The World*, Drury Lane, 1880, a melodrama by Paul Meritt, Henry Pettitt and Augustus Harris.

Drury Lane, after its decline as a classical theatre, found success as the home of spectacular melodrama under the management of Augustus Harris, 1879 to 1896, and his successor Arthur Collins, who remained in charge until 1923.

Harris often acted in and was part of his productions, which presented real life and incident on the stage, on a vast scale, starting a tradition of Drury Lane drama, eventually to become outmoded by the rise of the cinema.

347. Mary Anderson as Juliet and Fanny Stirling as the Nurse, Lyceum, 1884.

Mary Anderson, one of the great beauties of the era, presented seasons at the Lyceum during Irving's tours. Born in 1859, she retired in 1889 and died in 1940.

348. Tree as Falstaff and Robb Harwood as Nym in *Henry IV, Part* 1, Haymarket, 1889.

Tree became manager of the Haymarket in 1887 and remained there until his new theatre, Her Majesty's, was built in 1897.

349. Lily Langtry (1852–1929) as Cleopatra, Princess's, 1890.

The most famous of Society beauties, went on the stage in 1881. She went into management in 1890, taking over the Imperial, Westminster, in 1901, which she rebuilt.

350. Madge Kendal as Rosalind, St. James's, 1885, revived during Hare and the Kendals' management of the theatre.

Mrs. Kendal, a sister of T. W. Robertson, retired in 1908, only to reappear on rare occasions.

351. Charles Wyndham (1837–1919) and Mary Moore (1882–1931) in *She Stoops to Conquer*, Criterion, 1880, which theatre he managed from 1876. He built Wyndham's Theatre (1899) and the New (1903).

352. Alma Murray (1854–1913) as Beatrice Cenci in Shelley's *The Cenci*, Grand Theatre, Islington, 1886.

Though written in 1819 it was not staged until this production by the Shelley Society.

353. Mary Rorke and Charles Wyndham in H. J. Byron's *Fourteen Days*, Criterion, 1882.

354. Wilson Barrett (1847–1904) in Henry Arthur Jones's and Henry Herman's *The Silver King*, Princess's, 1882.

355. E. S. Willard, Annie Hughes and E. W. Garden in Henry Arthur Jones's *The Middleman*, Shaftesbury, 1889.

356. Interior of the Haymarket Theatre, as rebuilt by the Bancrofts, 1880, where they remained until they retired in 1885. For the first time the stage was completely surrounded by the proscenium, forming the "picture-frame stage" which has remained the accepted method of play production, despite many attempts to break its limitations. The reintroduction of the apron stage for classical plays came with Granville Barker, and only became reinstated at the Old Vic and Stratford in the 1930's.

357. Mr. and Mrs. Kendal with T. N. Wenman in Pinero's *The Squire*, St. James's, 1881.

Pinero (1855–1934), first an actor, wrote several successes before the famous series of Court Theatre farces. His first venture in the footsteps of Ibsen and the "New Drama," and what was then considered "unpleasant," was *The Profligate*, 1889. He went on to write the first serious English plays on social problems and revitalise our drama.

358. Stella Patrick Campbell and George Alexander in Pinero's *The Second Mrs. Tanqueray*, St. James's, 1893, which made the reputation of both playwright and actress.

359. Forbes Robertson (1853–1937) and Kate Rorke in *Lady Bountiful*, Garrick Theatre, 1891.

Pinero wrote *The Profligate* to inaugurate Hare's management of the newly built Garrick Theatre, 1889. *Lady Bountiful* followed. Forbes Robertson, who had been with Irving, was soon to join the ranks of the actor-managers at the Lyceum.

360. Stella Patrick Campbell (1865–1940) as Agnes in Pinero's *The Notorious Mrs. Ebbsmith*, Garrick, 1895. His second heroine in the New Drama.

361. *Liberty Hall*, a scene from R. C. Carton's play at the St. James's, 1892.

Carton, a minor "Society" dramatist, wrote numerous plays between 1885 and 1911. George Alexander (1858–1918), from Irving's Lyceum company, went into management at the St. James's in 1891. He soon established the theatre as the home of Society drama and comedy, impeccably presented for what Pinero termed "our Parish of St. James's." He remained at the theatre until his death.

The St. James's Theatre, built in 1835, was very unsuccessful during its early years. It was used by German and French companies through the 1840's. The Hare and Kendal's management gave the theatre its first successes and a reputation it has retained ever since.

362. *Trelawney of the "Wells,"* Court, 1898.

Pinero in this play paid his debt to T. W. Robertson by dramatising him as "Tom Wrench," struggling to write in a new style and to improve the status of his profession. It is his only "Period" play. It gave Irene Vanbrugh her first major success, as Rose.

By the '90's, photography had advanced sufficiently to be able to leave the "studio" and enter the theatre, and record for posterity plays as they were seen by contemporary audiences.

363. Janet Achurch (1864–1916) as Nora in *A Doll's House*, 1889.

Ibsen's play, written in 1878–79, was first produced at the Novelty Theatre in William Archer's translation. It was the first direct translation of Ibsen to be seen in London. The "Intellectual Drama" had arrived, and a path was opened for Shaw.

364. Alma Murray as Raina in *Arms and the Man*, Avenue Theatre, 1894.

Bernard Shaw's fourth play and his first appearance in the commercial theatre as a playwright and producer. His first play, *Widower's Houses*, begun in 1885 but laid aside, was finished for private production in 1892, by the newly formed Independent Theatre Society.

365. Winifred Fraser as Hedvig in *The Wild Duck*, Royalty, 1894.

Ibsen was first brought to the London stage through Archer's translations. Though produced for small coterie audiences, the influence of the plays was far-reaching.

366. Elizabeth Robbins as Hilda Wangel in *The Master Builder*, Trafalgar Square Theatre (later, Duke of York's), 1893. Janet Achurch and Elizabeth Robbins were the first of the "intellectual" actresses, whose pioneer work did much to establish the "New drama."

367. Lewis Waller, Charles Hawtrey and Julia Neilson in Wilde's *An Ideal Husband*, Haymarket, 1895.

368. George Alexander as John Worthing in Wilde's *The Importance of Being Earnest*, St. James's, 1895.

369. Marion Terry as Mrs. Erlynne in Wilde's *Lady Windermere's Fan*, St. James's, 1892. Alexander played Lord Darlington.

370. *Lady Windermere's Fan*, Lord Darlington's Rooms, Act III, St. James's, 1892.

Oscar Wilde (1856–1900) wrote three Society comedies, of which *Lady Windermere's Fan* was the first. While these conform to the established mode of the problem play, Wilde's wit and brilliant epigrams lift them out of the realms of similar plays of the era.

His *Importance of Being Earnest*, while it contains all the familiar ingredients of its day, transports them to the heights of parody, the result being the most brilliant comedy in the English language. His historical plays are of less importance.

371. *Walker, London*, Toole's Theatre, 1892. Sketch for the setting by Joseph Harker.

J. L. Toole, took the Folly Theatre in 1879, giving it his own name in 1882. Here was produced *Walker, London*, the first play by J. M. Barrie (1860–1937). The setting of a houseboat on the Thames was highly original in its day. His sentimental comedies, *The Professor's Love Story* (1892) and *The Little Minister* (1897), are also of the Victorian era, but his main output belongs to the twentieth century.

Toole's Theatre was closed in 1895, to become part of the Charing Cross Hospital.

372. *Romeo and Juliet*, Lyceum, 1895.

With this play Forbes Robertson went into management at the Lyceum, with Mrs. Patrick Campbell as his leading lady. Together they played in *The School for Scandal*, *Hamlet*, *Macbeth* and other productions.

Forbes Robertson followed in Irving's tradition of production until he retired in 1913, though he presented Shaw and other modern dramatists.

373. Forbes Robertson and Mrs. Patrick Campbell in *For the Crown*, Lyceum, 1896.

An adaptation by John Davidson of a romantic drama by Coppées.

374. Forbes Robertson as Hamlet, Lyceum, 1897.

The greatest Hamlet after Irving. A scholarly interpretation, still considered unsurpassed by the older playgoer. He last played it in 1913.

375. Frank Benson (1859–1939) as Hamlet, Globe, 1889.

He commenced his career with Irving in 1882 and formed his own company in 1883 which he maintained until 1929.

376. *Hamlet*, a William Poel production at Carpenters' Hall, 1900, with an all-male cast.

William Poel (1852–1934) commenced his experiments of staging Shakespeare's plays in the Elizabethan manner in 1881, when he produced *Hamlet* in the First Quarto version at St. George's Hall, following this with similar ventures with the Elizabethan Stage Society, which he had founded, until 1905. His work, completely at variance with the production methods of his day, found disciples and stimulated others in the commercial theatre to strive to free Shakespeare from the cumbersome trappings and the textual cuts made necessary by them, paving the way for our present methods.

377. *The Musketeers*, Her Majesty's Theatre, 1898.
Sydney Grundy's version of the Dumas novel.

Tree had great success at the Haymarket and took the old Opera House in the Haymarket, which had passed through many rebuildings since it was opened by Vanbrugh as the Queen's Theatre in 1705. On the site he built Her Majesty's Theatre, opening in 1897. Here he attempted to rival Irving in the magnificence of his productions, staging Shakespeare, modern plays and poetic drama until 1915. He continually revived his productions and virtually made His Majesty's into a national theatre with annual Shakespearean Festivals of his own and other actor-managers' productions.

378. Lewis Waller (1860–1915), Tree and Julia Neilson in *Hypatia*, Haymarket, 1893. Founded by Stuart Ogilvie on Charles Kingsley's novel.

379. Tree as Svengali in *Trilby*, Haymarket, 1895.
Paul Potter's adaptation of George Du Maurier's novel, the profits from which enabled him to build his new theatre.

380. Tree as Marc Antony in *Julius Caesar*, Her Majesty's, 1898.
His first Shakespeare revival at the new theatre, and one of his major successes.

381. *King John*, the Newstead Abbey scene, Her Majesty's, 1899.

Tree carried scenic effects to their utmost limit, sacrificing Shakespeare to the designer and producer. Though exceedingly popular with the playgoing public, many actors and producers were revolting against these methods, though under Tree there came a revival of the poetic drama, with the work of Stephen Phillips (1864–1915), made palatable to the public by Tree's lavish settings.

As an actor Tree was erratic, tiring of a part quickly—his mind working ahead on future projects.

382. William Terriss and W. L. Abingdon in *The Fatal Card*, Adelphi, 1894. A melodrama by Haddon Chambers and B. C. Stephenson. Abingdon was famous for his "villains."

383. George Alexander in *The Prisoner of Zenda*, St. James's, 1896. An adaptation of Anthony Hope's romantic Ruritanian novel by Edward Rose.

384. Wilson Barrett and Maud Jefferies in *The Sign of the Cross*, Lyric, 1896.
Barrett's own melodrama on a religious theme.

385. Martin Harvey and N. de Silva in *The Only Way*, Lyceum, 1899. Harvey's first venture into management and his greatest success.

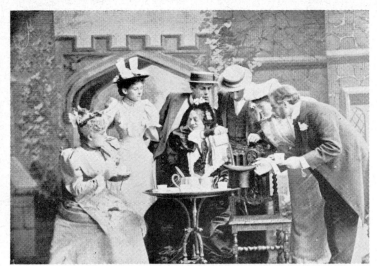

386. *Charley's Aunt*, Royalty, 1892. The famous farce by Brandon Thomas, with W. S. Penley as Lord Fancourt Babberley. It ran originally for 1,466 performances—a record for a play held until beaten by *Blithe Spirit*. Its Christmas revivals have become a ritual since 1901.

387. *Poor Mr. Potton*, Vaudeville Theatre, 1895. A farce by C. Hamlyn and H. M. Paull, in which Weedon Grossmith played the lead. He acted in many similar plays in a long career.

Farces of this nature were extremely popular at the turn of the century. The "New Woman" ready and waiting for emancipation was an easy target for satire.

388. *A Pair of Spectacles*, Garrick, 1895. Kate Rorke, John Hare and Philip Cunningham in Sydney Grundy's comedy.

Grundy (1848–1914) wrote numerous dramas and comedies in the style of the period, firmly resisting the "New Drama" and the influence of Ibsen, which he opposed and violently attacked. He denounced the emancipation of women in *The New Woman*, 1894.

389. *The Liars*, Criterion, 1897.

Henry Arthur Jones (1851–1931), who with Pinero did most to establish "Society drama," first wrote melodramas. He began to call for the renaissance of the English Drama in 1884. His plays: *The Dancing Girl* (1891), *The Case of Rebellious Susan* (1894), *Mrs. Dane's Defence* (1900) and many others written up to 1913, were to put his ideas into practice. He was a superb craftsman, but his plays have not outlived the society and the audiences about which and for whom he wrote.

390. *Under Milk Wood*, a verse play by Dylan Thomas, New Theatre, 1956.
Written for broadcasting, it was adapted with great success for theatrical presentation, and directed by Douglas Cleverdon and Edward Burnham with a setting by Michael Tangmar.

PART SIX

The Twentieth Century

(1901–1957)

QUEEN VICTORIA outlived the period to which she gave her name by only a year. The following nine years of the Edwardian era are, theatrically, but an extension of the "Renaissance of the Drama" born in the '90's. The remaining four years till the outbreak of war saw the new ideas gaining a foothold in the precincts of the Commercial theatre. Almost overnight the tick of the theatre clock was stopped, not to strike again until the 1930's, though faint chimes were heard from the provincial wilderness and suburban outposts, and the Alarm was continually being sounded in the many private play-producing Societies.

These Societies fostered the Intellectual Drama, trained actors, in newer methods and styles, gave the producer an opportunity to experiment and to find his feet. With Robertson, the author became his own producer; this method was followed by Pinero and Shaw. But a new breed of "Director" was to arise, either an actor or playwright and later sometimes a man unconnected with the practical side of the theatre, a man who would inter-

pret the work of a dramatist, living or dead, and impose his will on the actors, making himself completely responsible for the final effect achieved.

The play-producing Societies not only looked after the "New Drama" but were later to look into the past and revive long-forgotten classics. As tastes changed and more enlightened days dawned, the drama these Societies had fostered and kept alive moved into the pattern of general West End theatre fare. Their work done, some turned to the task of discovering new playwrights, others faded from the scene. The Club theatres which rose in the '20's took over their work. These often were the home of "Experimental" theatre and the "Expressionist" drama. After the Second World War economics forced many of these theatres to disappear, with no great loss to the drama. Those which have survived still are doing the work which inspired their inception, particularly in the presentation of plays which fail to pass the Censor but otherwise are of real worth.

One side of the Societies' work taken on by the

"other theatre" was the introduction of the Russian dramatists to this country. The plays of Chekhov were to have far-reaching effects on our native dramatists, and the plays themselves were eventually to find a place in the Commercial theatre. The Russian method of approach to acting, via the work of Stanislavsky began to have an influence on the actor's art through the producer. In America it took even a stronger hold, to produce what is now known as "The Method."

During Edwardian days the great actor-managers rose to their full glory. Tree carried on the work of Irving, though he flirted with the New tendencies—Ibsen and Shaw figured in his repertoire. He instituted a series of Matinée performances of unusual plays, and it is incredible to find the name of William Poel on the Committee of the 1910 Shakespeare Festival, as Poel's method represented the complete opposite of everything he stood for—though let it be recorded that Tree acted Hamlet in 1910 entirely in a tapestry background, and toyed with the idea of employing Gordon Craig for his 1911 *Macbeth*.

Craig's book, *The Art of the Theatre* published in 1905, put forward new methods of Design, Lighting and Production, some of which he had managed to bring to the theatre in London, though his influence through this and his following books was more felt on the Continent and in America, where his work bore the most fruit.

The other actor-managers continued along the lines which had established them in the public favour, but their world vanished with the War. Strangely enough, by the time it was over most of them had died. The post-war theatre had no place for the actor-manager and owner of his own theatre. Bricks and mortar passed into the hands of business syndicates.

Shaw, who had found his feet in the private Societies, became established in the favour of the intellectual play-goer in the public theatre by the work of the Vedrenne-Barker Seasons at the Court, and in the West End soon he was able to command an audience in the Commercial theatre. Audiences at last began to enjoy being made to think. The rest of his story, via the Malvern Festivals and constant "commercial" revivals, led to his plays becoming classics in his lifetime and part of the established repertory of the British theatre.

The new ideas bore fruit in the works of Galsworthy and many others—a return to the classical style of the Society "Comedy of Manners" is marked by the work of Somerset Maugham which spans the Edwardian and Post-War eras and links us with the new generation.

Before this new era was reached the War years had to be passed. Granville Barker, who had shown the way to the new enlightened production of Shakespeare in the years immediately preceding the War, had his work abruptly brought to a close. The new-found freedom of production and drama was carried on by the newly established provincial Repertory movement. The plays of

Shakespeare retired humbly to the newly founded Old Vic Company, where they were kept alive and found a new generation of devotees who were able to bring them back in triumph to the West End in the '30's. At last the texts of Shakespeare's plays were restored to their original glory, purged of the work of emendation and adaptation. The decline of elaborate scenic effect also allowed time for the whole text to be performed, and the plays often emerged unrecognisable in their completeness. The trend was seen when Benson performed *Hamlet* in its entirety at the Lyceum in 1900, though it took a matinée and evening performance. This seems the first recorded production of the whole play since Elizabethan days. The entire play was to become frequently seen at the Old Vic at one sitting from 1917.

The War years in the West End produced light entertainment—Spy plays, farces, romantic, "escapist" drama—little of lasting worth. With the coming of the '20's the Commercial theatre was filled with light comedies, the newly exploited "Detective" drama, "Thrillers" and Society comedies. Production and acting became more and more naturalistic. Gradually playwrights of worth emerged in the new mediums—Coward, Lonsdale, Van Druten and A. A. Milne—while Shakespeare had only occasional West End revivals. The Restoration and Georgian plays, brought to notice by the Societies, came again into public favour at the Lyric, Hammersmith, under Nigel Playfair. Melodrama once more reared its head, masked and newly disguised, in the plays of Edgar Wallace and his followers. A large number of expert professional dramatists arose, who could always be relied upon for a success—in a way which had made the late Victorian and Edwardian theatre prosperous. These dramatists extended and multiplied in the 1930's, adding R. C. Sherriff, J. B. Priestley, Emlyn Williams and Terence Rattigan to their ranks, followed by Peter Ustinov in the next decade.

With the return to the West End of the classical repertoire, mainly through the rise to popularity of John Gielgud, so theatre designers rose in power. Granville Barker had encouraged artists, as opposed to the scenic designer. Gradually there became scope for the work of wholetime theatrical designers of worth.

The Continent in the '20's, following in the footsteps of Gordon Craig, established "the New Movement in the Theatre," and with it the Expressionist Drama. Though seen here in the small Club theatres and occasionally in the West End, its ideas and methods took little root. Later, however, it was to return to London in triumph with the invasion of American plays since the '40's—in which country the new movement had been well digested, artistically developed and so made palatable to English audiences in the work of Thornton Wilder, Tennessee Williams and Arthur Miller.

The Second World War did not see a repetition of the

same theatre pattern as previously. Though new work was often light it was well written. The West End saw many magnificent revivals of the best of the Drama, and plays which in the past had not a large drawing power, achieved phenomenal success. A vast new audience was created by the tours of C.E.M.A. and later the Arts Council, at last the Government was interesting itself and subsidising the drama. The plays of Shakespeare, mainly with Old Vic Companies and at Stratford, gained a popularity with a larger public than ever before, though, it must be said, with the help of the reputation of actors gained in the world of cinema. After the War the new audiences, particularly in the outlying areas, drifted away and little could be done to consolidate the newly won ground. However, the post-war years saw the introduction of certain Civic theatres. It is to Shakespeare mainly that the "new audiences" have remained faithful. The post-war generation has continued to support the Old Vic, Stratford and the Bristol Old Vic. That strange phenomenon of recent years, the "bobby-soxer" seemed at one moment to be infiltrating from their own particular sphere into the classic theatre; though generally taken to be "fan" worship of a particular favourite, the thought has crossed the mind of some that the noisy outbursts could be for the Poet himself!

This century seems to have brought more drastic changes of taste to the theatre than any before. Perhaps because it is nearer to us we see all these new trends more clearly than those of previous centuries. Viewed at a distance, these changes can be summed up in another way:

At the start of the century playgoers went to see an actor: he was the Star attraction. The question would be: "Have you seen Tree, Waller or Alexander in their new play?" Soon it would become: "Have you seen the new Maugham, Coward or Lonsdale?" The play commanded the Star billing.

Next to command the top of the Bill was the Producer. He gradually imposed his personality on the public, and the question was: "Have you been to Komisarjevsky's, Guthrie's or Peter Brook's new production?"

The full significance of the battle for supreme command was reached recently when for a revival of a famous farce the largest billing went to the Stage Designer!

The theatre of today seems to have found a happy combination of all these contending elements, but with the unfortunate decline of the principal contributor—the playwright.

With the "discovery" of Psychology, a convenient means of "explanation" was put into the dramatist's hands, and a new form of "psychological drama" was born, which came to us mainly via America. The influence of this new approach spread into most dramas: almost overnight the primary colours of character drawing passed into the shadows. Producers have often tried to graft this new approach on to plays written before the era of its under-standing—mostly with fatal results. "Overtones and undertones" have broken the back of many a revival. To our eyes, accustomed as they now are to the psychiatrist and his methods, a whole era of drama has become completely dated and outmoded, though it can still be made palatable if producers, actors and audience clear their minds of the revelations of the consulting room.

A curious phenomenon of the post-Second World War theatre was the emergence of the Verse Drama to favour in the works of T. S. Eliot, Christopher Fry and Dylan Thomas. The form had passed gradually from the theatre in mid-Victorian times—to emerge shyly with Tennyson, made actable by Irving, and to have a short resurrection in Edwardian days through Stephen Phillips and other lesser poets. But for Flecker's *Hassan*, produced in 1923 by Basil Dean, the poets did not again take the stage until the success of *Murder in the Cathedral*, in 1935. From a slow start the place of the modern poet in the theatre has been regained to a great extent.

In the last ten years our theatre has seen an influx of plays from France: Giraudoux, Sartre and Anouilh have proved the contemporary worth of the French drama, when seen in indirect translations.

British professional playwrights have fallen into a slough of despond. Some have ceased to write; others remain bound to the period in which they achieved their greatest success. Some write all too seldom, when before they were regular in their output. New names have emerged and after one or two successes, vanished again into limbo. The cry of the critic has been continuously for new plays. To try and meet this demand writers from other fields have been disastrously recruited to the theatre. Amateurs, as opposed to the erstwhile professional playwright who knew and understood the technique of his craft, have been prematurely encouraged. The cry is that what is new must be encouraged, however immature.

It is often forgotten that the theatre is a place of entertainment: even Shaw, who shook playgoers and made them think, never forgot this, and sugared his pill. The serious modern playwright must not give the public only significant drama of the sordid surroundings of modern life, but enlarge his canvas to satisfy the tastes of the less angry playgoers.

This History has shown that the drama undergoes periods when it is unaccountably in decline. Are we now in a similar plight, as we move towards what looks to be again the dull '60's, and awaiting the coming of a new Tom Robertson? Have all the tricks of the "New Drama" been worn threadbare, and is something entirely new needed to revitalise the drama?

On the acting side, we have players who will take their place in history beside the greatest names of the past, in the best traditions of the English stage. Those who love the theatre know it can never die. It only sleeps at times, awaiting the call to awake with new vigour.

391. Martin Harvey and N. de Silva in *The Breed of the Treshams*, Lyric, 1905 — a romantic drama by John Rutherford.

Cloak and dagger dramas had a great vogue in the Edwardian era.

392. Fred Terry and Julia Neilson in *The Scarlet Pimpernel*, New, 1905. Montague Barstow's version of Baroness Orczy's novel. One of the many husband-and-wife actor-manager partnerships in the theatre.

393. Grace Lane and Lewis Waller in *Monsieur Beaucaire*, Comedy, 1902. Booth Tarkington's powder-patch romance revived seven times by Waller until 1907. His admirers formed a "Keen on Waller" club.

394. Evelyn Millard and Henry Ainley in *Paolo and Francesca*, St. James's, 1902. Stephen Phillips' verse play, for which a fashion arose in the early years of the century.

395. *Ulysses* at His Majesty's Theatre, 1902. The Killing of the Suitors in Stephen Phillips' poetic drama.

Tree also produced his *Herod*, 1900, and *Nero*, 1906. Also at the Adelphi under Otho Stewart, in the first decade of the century, verse drama reached a popularity which was not to recur until the coming of T. S. Eliot and Christopher Fry.

396. Martin Harvey as Œdipus in the spectacular production by Max Reinhardt at the Royal Opera House, Covent Garden, 1912, where he revived it again, 1936.

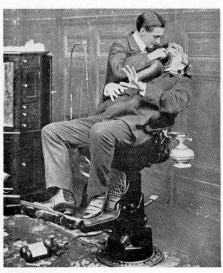

397. *You Never Can Tell*, Court, 1906. Henry Ainley and Edmund Gurney in Shaw's first public success.

398. *Captain Brassbound's Conversion*, Court, 1906. Frederick Kerr and Ellen Terry in Shaw's play.

399. *Caesar and Cleopatra*, Savoy, 1907. Gertrude Elliott and Forbes Robertson in Shaw's play.

400. *Major Barbara*, Court, 1905. Louis Calvert and Granville Barker in Act II of Shaw's play.

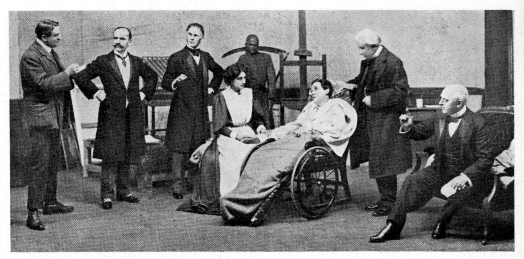

401. *The Doctor's Dilemma*, Court, 1906, with Lillah McCarthy and Granville Barker.
    The Vedrenne-Barker season at the Court lasted from 1904 to 1906. It brought Shaw's plays to a wider public and established him as the major dramatist of the day.

402. *Pygmalion*, His Majesty's, 1914.
    Edmund Gurney, Mrs. Patrick Campbell and Beerbohm Tree in the first production in English of Shaw's play. It established him in the commercial theatre and has remained his most popular play.
    Bernard Shaw (1856–1950), after achieving only private productions, except for *Arms and the Man*, from 1892 until the Court seasons, at last was recognised in the West End. Playgoers were now being made to think as well as being entertained.

403. *Quality Street*. Ellaline Terriss and Seymour Hicks in J. M. Barrie's play, Vaudeville, 1902. A partnership also famous in Musical Comedy.

404. *Peter Pan*. Nina Boucicault as Peter, Hilda Trevelyan as Wendy and Gerald Du Maurier as Hook, in Barrie's fairy play, Duke of York's, 1904.

405. *The Admirable Crichton*. H. B. Irving and Irene Vanbrugh in Barrie's fantasy, Duke of York's, 1902.

406. *Beauty and the Barge*. Mary Brough and Cyril Maude in W. W. Jacobs' comedy, New, 1904.

407. *Typhoon*. Mabel Hackney with Laurence Irving in his own play, Haymarket, 1913. Henry Irving's two sons, H. B. and Laurence, both became successful actor-managers.

408. *Raffles*. Gerald Du Maurier and Laurence Irving in an adaptation of E. W. Hornung's novel, Comedy, 1906.

409. *An Englishman's Home*, Wyndham's, 1909. Guy Du Maurier's play, anticipating the consequences of a foreign invasion of England, which created a sensation in Edwardian days.

410. *Romeo and Juliet*. Matheson Lang and Nora Kerin, Lyceum, 1908. Presented in a season of costume dramas for a popular audience. Lang—an old Bensonian—made his name during the season and soon joined the ranks of the actor-managers.

411. *Henry V*. Lewis Waller and Sarah Brooke, Lyceum, 1900. Waller's most famous Shakespearean role, revived many times.

412. *Measure for Measure*. Oscar Asche and Lily Brayton, Adelphi, 1906.

413. *Henry VIII*. The Trial scene, with Arthur Bourchier and Violet Vanbrugh in Tree's production, His Majesty's, 1910. He himself played Wolsey.

414. *Antony and Cleopatra*. Beerbohm Tree, Basil Gill and Constance Collier, His Majesty's, 1906. Tree at his height and his most spectacular.

415. *Dante*. Henry Irving in Sardou's play—his last new production, Drury Lane, 1903.

Harley Granville Barker (1877–1946) first appeared as an actor in London from 1892. He became associated with the Stage Society in 1900, appearing as Marchbanks in *Candida*. He quickly became the prime mover in their work of establishing the New Drama in the theatre. He took the Court Theatre with J. E. Vedrenne in 1904, where he remained till 1907. Here he produced Greek drama and worthwhile plays by contemporary dramatists —Galsworthy, Hankin, Housman, and eleven by Shaw, three of which were especially written for this theatre. He transferred his work to the West End for seasons at the Savoy, Haymarket, Kingsway and St. James's, in association with his wife Lillah McCarthy, who was the leading lady in many of his productions. In him Shaw found the ideal man to carry out his methods and to stage his plays.

416. *Twelfth Night*, Savoy, 1912. Settings and costumes by Norman Wilkinson.

417. *The Winter's Tale*, Savoy, 1912. Settings by Norman Wilkinson. Costumes by Albert Rothenstein.

Barker also wrote numerous plays, of which the most important are *The Voysey Inheritance* (1905), *Waste* (1907) and *The Madras House* (1910). He is the first of the modern "Directors"—the actor-manager had usually staged his own production, and with the coming of the "New Drama" the playwright had gone into the theatre himself to produce —an example set by Tom Robertson in the '60's. Shaw was responsible for the production of the majority of his plays: Barker heralds the arrival in the theatre of the Director, as we understand the term today.

In 1912 he turned his attention to Shakespeare and produced *Twelfth Night* in a manner which startled his contemporaries. He abolished the heavy scenery and trappings, restored the text, playing it with a speed and fluency then unheard of—except in the experiments of William Poel. Barker called upon artists of repute to come into the theatre and design his settings and costumes. His work was cut short by the coming of the War, and it took nearly another twenty years for his production methods to become generally accepted in the West End. Barker himself retired from active work in the theatre in 1920, to write his monumental Prefaces to Shakespeare.

418. *A Midsummer Night's Dream*, Savoy, 1914. Settings and costumes by Norman Wilkinson.

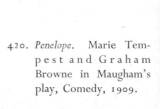

419. *Lady Frederick*. Graham Browne and Ethel Irving in W. Somerset Maugham's first success, Court, 1907.

420. *Penelope*. Marie Tempest and Graham Browne in Maugham's play, Comedy, 1909.

422. *Doormats*, by Hubert Henry Davies. Alfred Bishop, Gerald Du Maurier, Dawson Millward, Nina Boucicault and Marie Löhr, Wyndham's, 1912. Produced by Du Maurier in a typical realistic setting.
Davies wrote numerous Society comedies, of which *The Mollusc* is the best known.

421. *The Woman in the Case*. Violet Vanbrugh and Grace Lane in Clyde Fitch's Society drama, Garrick, 1909.

423. *His House in Order*. George Alexander and Irene Vanbrugh in Pinero's play, St. James's, 1906.

424. *The Walls of Jericho*. Violet Vanbrugh and Arthur Bourchier in Alfred Sutro's play, Garrick, 1904.

The Edwardian era was rich in Society dramatists who could expertly exploit the topical problems of the day, in a manner palatable to their audiences.

Maugham, after many difficulties, came to fame with *Lady Frederick*. Immediately, others of his plays were produced and he achieved the unique feat of having four running in London at the same time.

Alfred Sutro (1863–1933) provided a number of successes for Arthur Bourchier's management of the Garrick Theatre and for George Alexander at the St. James's, where *Builder of Bridges* was produced in 1908. Pinero continued to write and some of his best remembered works date from the Edwardian era: *His House in Order*, *Mid-Channel* (1909). His last play was in 1932, but by then he had lost his hold on the public.

Novelists have always been attracted to the theatre, but the necessary restrictions of dramatic form have prevented them from success in this medium, though collaboration with a playwright who understood the technical craft of the theatre often achieved the result. Edward Knoblock was in great demand for such services in his long career; then he had successes on his own account, including *Kismet* (1911).

Jerome K. Jerome—actor, novelist and playwright—wrote many successes but is best remembered for his play of the mysterious stranger who visits a Bloomsbury boarding-house and reforms the lives of the inhabitants.

John Galsworthy (1867–1933), first a novelist, wrote *The Silver Box* for the Vedrenne-Barker management at the Court in 1906.

425. *The Passing of the Third Floor Back.* Haidée Wright, Forbes Robertson and Gertrude Elliott, in Jerome K. Jerome's modern Morality play, St. James's, 1908.

426. *Milestones*, a play of three generations, by Arnold Bennett and Edward Knoblock, Royalty, 1912.

He followed this with *Joy* and *Strife*, which established him among the foremost dramatists of the day. Among his other plays, *Justice* (1910), *The Skin Game* (1920) and *Loyalties* (1922), are all on problems of existing conditions in need of reform. Though written in a masterly style, the very topicality of the themes has prevented them remaining alive in the theatre.

Justice was produced during the Charles Frohman repertory season at the Duke of York's, 1910, a courageous attempt to bring a repertory season of new plays to the West End, works by Shaw, Granville Barker and Barrie were also produced, but the venture unfortunately did not prosper, with the exception of a revival of Pinero's *Trelawney of the "Wells."*

427. *Strife*, John Galsworthy's play of industrial dispute, Comedy, 1913. The play was first produced in 1909, one of the most successful of his series of similar plays.

428. *Mr. Wu.* Lilian Braithwaite and Matheson Lang in Vernon and Owen's Anglo-Chinese play, Strand, 1913. One of Lang's most successful plays and creations.

429. *Diana of Dobson's.* C. M. Hallard and Lena Ashwell in Cicely Hamilton's play of the problems of a shop assistant, by a woman dramatist, Kingsway, 1908.

430. *When Knights Were Bold.* Wyndham's, 1907. Audrey Ford and James Welch in the farce by Charles Marlowe (Harriet Jay). A popular Christmas revival for many years.

431. *Bunty Pulls the Strings.* A Scottish comedy by Graham Moffat, Playhouse, 1911. It had a long run and paved the way for many similar dialect comedies.

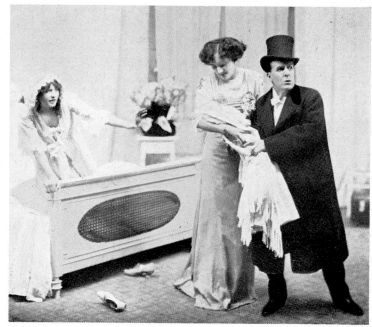

433. *Baby Mine.* Iris Hoey, Lilias Waldergrave and Weedon Grossmith in a farce by Margaret Mayo, Criterion, 1911.

432. *The Whip.* The Train Crash in Cecil Raleigh and Henry Hamilton's sporting drama, Drury Lane, 1909. Typical of the series of "Autumn Melodrama" at the Lane.

The theatre at this time provided not only Society dramas, but the comedies and farces moved into the best circles. Dialect plays became accepted via the Manchester school of dramatists and their followers. Women dramatists again began to write for the theatre, though still often hiding their identity under a male name—even though it was the age of the suffragette. At Drury Lane a pantomime and a new drama each autumn kept the theatre full, providing sensational spectacles with horse races and earthquakes, soon to become the province of the cinema.

434. *The Shewing-Up of Blanco Posnet* at the Abbey Theatre, Dublin, 1909.
Shaw's "Sermon in crude melodrama," banned from the London stage, was produced at the Abbey Theatre founded by Annie Horniman, though by this time it was being run by Lady Gregory and W. B. Yeats. The Irish Players first came to London in 1904, bringing the work of the Irish dramatists to a wider public.

435. *Back to Methuselah*, Part 1 of Shaw's Cycle in Five Parts, first produced in England at the Birmingham Repertory Theatre in 1923, and by them in London the following year, with settings by Paul Shelving.

The rise of the Provincial Repertory Theatre is a feature of the pre-Great War era. Miss Horniman, who had helped financially to establish the Abbey Theatre, Dublin, in 1904, opened the Gaiety Theatre, Manchester, in 1908 and established a repertory company. Liverpool was founded in 1911, with Basil Dean; Glasgow by Alfred Waring in 1909. The Birmingham Repertory Theatre was founded in 1913 by Barry Jackson, who built his own theatre. These theatres not only produced the best work of the established "New" playwrights but introduced many foreign works to this country and revived the classics. They provided an excellent training school and sent a steady stream of producers, actors and playwrights to the West End.

Some of the original companies still flourish and many others have taken up the work—not merely reproducing West End successes week by week—but experimenting in new fields.

436. *Hindle Wakes*, by Stanley Houghton, 1912. The most successful play from the Manchester school of dramatists, bred by Miss Horniman and her repertory company at the Gaiety Theatre, Manchester. These plays of North Country life marked a new style of naturalistic playwriting, which was to have far-reaching influence.

437. *An Enemy of the People*, Ibsen's play at the Liverpool Repertory Theatre, 1913. The repertory companies brought to the provinces the plays of the "New School" and interesting revivals. Their pioneer work, which still continues, did much to establish worthwhile plays with a public which was not reached by the commercial touring theatre.

438. *The Man Who Stayed at Home*, Royalty, 1914. Ruth Mackay and Denis Eadie in a spy play by Lechmere Worrall and Harold Terry. Dennis Eadie was associated with J. E. Vedrenne in the management of the Royalty Theatre for many years.

439. *The Dynasts*, an adaptation for the stage of Thomas Hardy's epic play, by Granville Barker, Kingsway, 1914. Barker, who produced the play, made use of a fore-stage in a setting by Norman Wilkinson.

440. *Abraham Lincoln*, Lyceum, 1921. William Rea and Felix Aylmer in John Drinkwater's play, first seen at the Birmingham Repertory, 1918.

441. *A Temporary Gentleman*, New Oxford Theatre, 1919. H. F. Maltby's play of the problem of the returning soldier.

442. *Tilly of Bloomsbury*, Apollo, 1919. Ian Hay's comedy of the clash of families with different backgrounds.

The wartime theatre mainly provided light entertainment—farces and light comedies thriving—the biggest successes being those on the musical stage, with revue and musical comedy. Shakespeare virtually disappeared from the West End, returning only spasmodically during the 1920's; it found its home at the Old Vic from 1914. The latter end of the period saw the rise of the "Thriller" which was to reach its peak with Edgar Wallace. Though certain managers strove to present intelligent plays, it was mainly in the repertories that the best work was to be found.

443. *The Naughty Wife*, Playhouse, 1918. A comedy by Frederick Jackson; with Ellis Jeffreys, Charles Hawtrey and Gladys Cooper, who was associated with management of this theatre from 1917 to 1933.

444. *Romance*, Duke of York's, 1915. Owen Nares and Doris Keane in Edward Sheldon's romantic drama. It had a run of 1,049 performances.

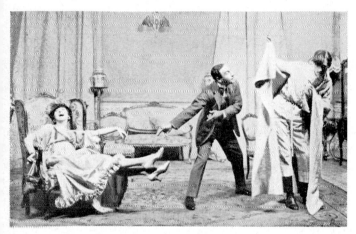

445. *A Little Bit of Fluff*, by Walter Ellis, Criterion, 1915. One of the War's long runs of 1,241 performances; with Ruby Miller, George Desmond and Ernest Thesiger.

446. *The Voice from the Minaret*, Globe, 1919. Arthur Wontner and Marie Löhr in Robert Hichens' play, produced under Marie Löhr's own management.

447. *The Thirteenth Chair*, Duke of York's, 1917. Mrs. Patrick Campbell (centre) in Bayard Veiller's thriller.

The actor-manager vanished from London with the War, though actress-managers once again arose at the Playhouse and the Globe. The Playhouse had originally been the Avenue Theatre, opened in 1882—rebuilt and rechristened by Cyril Maude in 1907 after he finished his management of the Haymarket. The Playhouse still stands, though not in use as a theatre. The Globe, opened as the Hicks in 1906, is still one of London's most successful theatres.

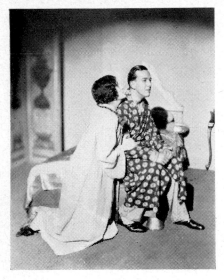

448. *The Vortex*. Lilian Braithwaite and Noël Coward in his own play, Royalty, 1924.

449. *The Gold Diggers*, Lyric, 1926. Ian Hunter, Fred Kerr and Tallulah Bankhead in Avery Hopwood's comedy. Tallulah Bankhead epitomised the "Gay '20's" and was seen "dressed and undressed" in many similar plays.

450. *The First Mrs. Fraser*, Haymarket, 1929. Marie Tempest and Henry Ainley in St. John Ervine's play.

451. *Spring Cleaning*, St. Martin's, 1925. The sensational Dinner scene in Frederick Lonsdale's Society comedy.

452. *Our Betters*, Globe, 1923, W. Somerset Maugham's comedy of morals, first seen in America in 1917.

453. *Outward Bound*, Garrick, 1923. Sutton Vane's fantasy, which has remained popular to this day, with Diana Hamilton, William Stack and Stanley Lathbury.

454. *Escape*, Ambassadors, 1926. Nicholas Hannen, Austin Trevor and Stafford Hilliard in Galsworthy's play of suspense on Dartmoor.

455. *And So To Bed*, Queen's, 1926. Yvonne Arnaud and Edmund Gwenn in J. B. Fagan's Pepysian play.

456. *Saint Joan*, New, 1924. Sybil Thorndike in Shaw's greatest play. It ran for 244 performances and has had eight revivals in London.

457. *The Way of the World*, Lyric, Hammersmith, 1924. Edith Evans and Robert Loraine in Nigel Playfair's production.

458. *Henry VIII*, Empire, 1925. The Trial scene. Sybil Thorndike played Queen Katherine in Lewis Casson's production, in a setting by Charles Ricketts. Cardinal Wolsey was played by Lyall Swete and Henry VIII by Norman V. Norman.

459. *Hamlet*, Kingsway, 1925. Barry Jackson's Modern Dress production, directed by H. K. Ayliff in Paul Shelving's settings. Colin Keith-Johnson played Hamlet.

460. *The Man With a Load of Mischief*, Haymarket, 1925. Ashley Duke's comedy, with Fay Compton and Frank Cellier.

461. *Hassan*, His Majesty's, 1923. James Elroy Flecker's verse play. Produced by Basil Dean. Henry Ainley played the title role.

462. *The Ringer*, Wyndham's, 1926. Leslie Faber and Dorothy Dickson in Edgar Wallace's "thriller."

463. *The Adding Machine*, Court, 1928. Elmer Rice's Expressionist cosmic drama.

464. *The Ghost Train*, St. Martin's, 1925. Mary Clare and Vincent Holman in Arnold Ridley's railway "thriller."

465. *The Fourth Wall*, Haymarket, 1928. A. A. Milne's play of detection. Nora Swinburne and Jack Hobbs, centre.

466. *Rookery Nook*, Aldwych, 1926. Ben Travers' second farce in the famous series at this theatre. For thirteen years farces with almost the same team: Tom Walls, Ralph Lynn, Robertson Hare, Mary Brough and Winifred Shotter, had phenomenal success.

467. *The Farmer's Wife*, Court, 1924. Maud Gill and Melville Cooper in Eden Philpotts' Devonshire comedy. Originally produced at the Birmingham Repertory, it was brought to London by Barry Jackson during his management at the Court, 1924–1928, and it ran for nearly three years.

468. *The Silver Tassie*, Apollo, 1929. Sean O'Casey's play of the Great War. The setting for the Second Act was by Augustus John. O'Casey's plays were mostly seen in the productions of the Irish Players.

469. *Journey's End*, Savoy, 1929. Colin Clive and Maurice Evans in R. C. Sherriff's War play.

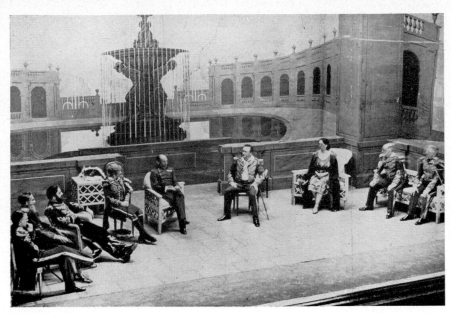

470. *The Apple Cart*, Malvern Festival, 1929. Shaw's political extravaganza, though written for the First Festival, was originally produced in Warsaw. It came to London the same year. At the First Festival were also played *Back to Methuselah*, *Heartbreak House* and *Caesar and Cleopatra*. Paul Shelving was responsible for most of the setting and costumes at the Festivals.

471. Barry Jackson as Chorus in Marlowe's *Doctor Faustus*, Malvern, 1934. One of his rare stage appearances.

The Malvern Festival was founded by Barry Jackson in 1929. Its original aim was to present the plays of Bernard Shaw, to whom it was dedicated. The Company was that of the Birmingham Repertory Theatre. The old Malvern Assembly Room was reconstructed as a theatre. Twenty-one of Shaw's plays were presented between 1929 and 1949, most of them were English premières, and two: *Geneva* (1938) and *In Good King Charles's Golden Days*, were world premières.

In 1931 the Festival enlarged its scope to include new plays by other authors and revivals, with a special Company engaged for the season. For the next two seasons the plays selected covered the History of English Drama from the earliest times.

Among the plays by contemporary authors first seen at the Festival were *The Barretts of Wimpole Street* by Rudolph Besier (1930), *A Sleeping Clergyman* by James Bridie (1933), *Music at Night* by J. B. Priestley (1938) and *What Say They?* by James Bridie (1939).

In 1925 Barry Jackson received a knighthood for his services to the theatre. He was director of the Shakespeare Festival, Stratford-upon-Avon, from 1945 to 1948.

472. *The Simpleton of the Unexpected Isles*. Shaw's contribution to the 1935 Festival. Though previously produced in New York the same year, the play was not seen in London until 1945, during Alec Clunes' management of the Arts Theatre. The setting and costumes at Malvern were designed by Marian Spencer.

473. *What Say They?*, Malvern, 1939. Besides Shaw, other famous dramatists had their plays first produced at the Festival, which continued until the outbreak of the Second World War. There have only been two Festivals since, in 1949, when *Buoyant Billions* was produced, and *Caesar and Cleopatra* for the Shaw Centenary, 1956.

474. *Macbeth*. Frank Benson and his Company at the Stratford Festival, 1903. Constance Benson played Lady Macbeth.

475. *Love's Labour's Lost*, Stratford Festival, 1934. Produced by W. Bridges-Adams, with a setting by Aubrey Hammond.

476. *The Comedy of Errors*, Stratford Festival, 1938. Komisarjevsky's production, for which he also designed the costumes and settings. This producer did much to introduce Chekhov to the public by his work at the Barnes theatre.

478. *Titus Andronicus*, Shakespeare Festival, 1955. Peter Brook's production, with his own costumes, settings and music. Seen in London at the Stoll in 1957.

477. *Much Ado About Nothing*, Stratford Festival, 1950. John Gielgud's production with Mariano Andreu's costumes and settings. First produced in 1949 with a different cast. It was seen in London at the Phoenix in 1952 and at the Palace in 1955.

The first Shakespeare Memorial Theatre, Stratford-upon-Avon, was opened in 1879, and Festivals have been given annually ever since, except for 1917 and 1918.

From 1886 to 1916 the productions were those of Frank Benson and his Company. The old theatre was burnt down in 1926, and the Festivals continued in a converted cinema until the New Theatre was opened in 1933.

In recent years the Company has attained a world-wide reputation and gives a seven-month season.

479. *The Tempest*, Open Air Theatre, 1934, with Leslie French and John Drinkwater. Robert Atkins was responsible for many productions in Regent's Park.

480. *The Rose Without a Thorn*, Duchess, 1932. Angela Baddeley and Frank Vosper in Clifford Bax's play.

481. *The Barretts of Wimpole Street*, Queen's, 1930. Cedric Hardwicke and Gwen Ffrangcon Davies in Rudolph Besier's play.

482. *Twelfth Night*, New, 1932. The "Black and White" production by Robert Atkins, with settings by Molly McArthur and Richard Santhem and costumes by John Gower Parks.

483. *Murder in the Cathedral*, Mercury, 1935. The first production of T. S. Eliot's historical verse play, with Robert Speaight. The Mercury became the home of verse drama.

484. *Richard of Bordeaux*, New, 1933. Gordon Daviot's historical play. with John Gielgud, Gwen Ffrangcon Davies, Barbara Dillon and Francis Lister. Designed by Motley.

485. *Hamlet*, New, 1934. John Gielgud in his own production, with Howieson Culff and Jack Hawkins. Designed by Motley. This was Gielgud's second *Hamlet,* he last played the part at the Haymarket, 1944.

486. *Private Lives*, Phoenix, 1930. Adrianne Allen, Noël Coward, Gertrude Lawrence and Laurence Olivier in Coward's play. The first production at the newly built theatre.

487. *Whiteoaks*, Little, 1936. Nancy Price as Gran in the People's National Theatre production of Mazo de la Roche's play.

488. *The Way to Treat a Woman*, Duke of York's, 1930. Marion Lorne, George Tully, Aubrey Smith and Cathleen Nesbitt in Walter Hackett's comedy.

489. *Proscenium*, Globe, 1933. Ivor Novello in his own play, with Keneth Kent and Fay Compton. Novello's comedies include *Fresh Fields*, *Full House* and *Party*.

490. *Late Night Final*, Phoenix, 1931. Five stages in action at one time. The theatre's challenge to the cinema in a play by Louis Wietzenkorn, dealing with the inside story of a sensational newspaper.

491. *Quiet Wedding*, Wyndham's, 1938. Frank Lawton and Elizabeth Allan in Esther McCracken's family comedy.

492. *The Corn is Green*, Duchess, 1938. Sybil Thorndike with Emlyn Williams in his own partly auto-biographical play of a Welsh miner.

493. *Victoria Regina*, Lyric, 1937. Pamela Stanley and Carl Esmond in Laurence Housman's play, designed by Rex Whistler.

494. *The Importance of Being Earnest*, Globe, 1939. Gwen Ffrangcon Davies, John Gielgud and Edith Evans in Gielgud's production of Wilde's play.

495. *Pride and Prejudice*, St. James's, 1936. Helen Jerome's dramatisation of Jane Austen's novel, with settings and costumes by Rex Whistler.

496. *Mourning Becomes Electra*, Westminster, 1937. Laura Cowie and Beatrix Lehmann in Eugene O'Neill's play.

497. *Johnson Over Jordan*, New, 1939. Ralph Richardson in J. B. Priestley's parable play.

498. *The Seagull*, New, 1936. Edith Evans and John Gielgud (centre) in his production of Chekhov's play, designed by Motley. In his season at the Queen's theatre in 1938, Gielgud also produced *The Three Sisters*.

499. Ernest Milton as Hamlet, Old Vic, 1925.

500. Robert Atkins as Sir Toby Belch in *Twelfth Night*, Old Vic, 1924.

501. John Gielgud as Hamlet, Old Vic, 1930.

502. *The Country Wife*, Old Vic, 1936. Iris Hoey, Edith Evans and Eileen Peel.

503. *Henry VIII*, The Trial scene, Old Vic, 1933. Charles Laughton as Henry VIII, Flora Robson as Queen Katherine and Robert Farquharson as Wolsey, in Tyrone Guthrie's production. The décor for this production was part of the Ricketts' sets designed for Lewis Casson's production at the Empire in 1925.

Lilian Baylis succeeded her aunt, Emma Cons, as manageress of the Old Vic in 1912. At first only concerts and opera were given, but in 1914 she introduced Shakespearean plays. A permanent Company was soon founded, and plays and opera alternated. She rebuilt Sadlers Wells in 1931, which building housed the Opera and Ballet Company from 1934.

504. *A Midsummer Night's Dream*, Old Vic, 1937. Tyrone Guthrie's production with Ralph Richardson, Vivien Leigh, Robert Helpmann and Gordon Miller. The settings were by Motley, and Mendelssohn's full score was used in a re-creation of a production of the date of the music. It was revived again in the following year with changes of cast.

Early directors of the Old Vic Company were Ben Greet, Robert Atkins and Harcourt Williams. By 1923 the theatre had presented all the plays in the First Folio, besides the first English production of Ibsen's *Peer Gynt* and other notable revivals. From the Company came many who were to achieve fame in the West End, and eventually it was to attract West End actors to its company for seasons. Under the direction of Tyrone Guthrie (1933–34) the productions began to attract a wider public than had hitherto made the pilgrimage across the river.

505. *Richard III*, Old Vic Company, New Theatre, 1944. Ralph Richardson and Laurence Olivier. The New Theatre was the Old Vic's wartime home.

506. *Henry IV, Part 1*, Old Vic Company, New Theatre, 1945. Ralph Richardson as Falstaff, Joyce Redman as Doll and Sybil Thorndike as Mistress Quickly.

507. *The School for Scandal*, Old Vic Company, New Theatre, 1949. Terence Morgan, Vivien Leigh, Laurence Olivier and Peter Cushing. Settings designed by Cecil Beaton.

508. *Tamburlaine*, Old Vic, 1951. Donald Wolfit in Tyrone Guthrie's production of Marlowe's play. Setting and costumes by Leslie Hurrey.

During the War, while the Old Vic theatre itself was out of use through blitz damage, the Company reached its peak of success at the New Theatre. Foreign tours gave the Company a world-wide reputation which it has maintained. They returned to the Old Vic in 1950. Since 1953, under the régime of Hugh Hunt, Tyrone Guthrie and Michael Benthall, the theatre has become established as what is to all intents and purposes our National Theatre.

509. *Hamlet*, Old Vic, 1953. The first production in the "Five Year Plan" to present all the plays of Shakespeare in the First Folio. Hamlet, Richard Burton; Ophelia, Claire Bloom; Gertrude, Fay Compton and Claudius, Laurence Hardy. Produced by Michael Benthall, designed by Kenneth Rowell.

510. *Blithe Spirit*, Piccadilly, 1941. Noël Coward's "improbable" farce, with Kay Hammond, Margaret Rutherford and Cecil Parker. It ran for a record of 1,997 performances.

511. *Old Acquaintance*, Apollo, 1941. Edith Evans and Marian Spencer in John Van Druten's comedy.

512. *The Man Who Came to Dinner*, Savoy, 1941. Moss Hart and Kaufman's comedy, with Coral Browne, Edward Cooper and Robert Morley. One of the many American plays introduced to London by Firth Shephard.

513. *The Duke in Darkness*, St. James's, 1942. Leslie Banks and Michael Redgrave in Patrick Hamilton's play.

514. *Flare Path*, Apollo, 1942. Terence Rattigan's play of the Air Force in wartime. His other plays include *French Without Tears*, *The Winslow Boy* and *The Deep Blue Sea*.

515. *Arsenic and Old Lace*, Strand, 1942. Lilian Braithwaite, Fred Beck and Mary Jerrold in Joseph Kesselring's macabre comedy which ran for 1,337 performances.

516. *Love for Love*, Phoenix, 1943. John Gielgud's production of Congreve's play. Designed by Rex Whistler.

517. *The Constant Couple*, Arts, 1943. Alec Clunes and Dorothy Primrose in Farquhar's comedy.

518. *There Shall Be No Night*, Aldwych, 1943. Robert Sherwood's play of a wartime invasion, with Muriel Pavlow, Lynn Fontanne, Frederick Lloyd and Alfred Lunt. "The Lunts" are a famous partnership on both sides of the Atlantic.

519. *The White Devil*, Duchess, 1947. Robert Helpmann and Margaret Rawlings in Webster's play.

520. *The Lady's Not for Burning*, Globe, 1949. John Gielgud's production of Christopher Fry's verse play. Designed by Oliver Messel. The play was first seen at the Arts Theatre the previous year with Alec Clunes.

521. *Don't Listen, Ladies!*, St. James's, 1948. Ada Reeve and Francis Lister in an adaptation from the French of Sasha Guitry.

522. *Daphne Laureola*, Wyndham's, 1949. Peter Williams, Edith Evans and Peter Finch in James Bridie's greatest success.

523. *A Streetcar Named Desire*, Aldwych, 1949. Vivien Leigh in Tennessee Williams' play.

524. *The Cocktail Party*, New, 1950. Alison Leggatt, Rex Harrison and Ian Hunter in T. S. Eliot's psychological verse play.

525. *The Holly and the Ivy*, Duchess Theatre, 1950. Wynyard Browne's play of vicarage life.

526. *Ring Round the Moon*, Globe, 1950. Christopher Fry's adaptation of Anouilh's play. Directed by Peter Brook, and designed by Oliver Messell.

527. *The River Line*, Lyric, Hammersmith, 1952. Charles Morgan's play of the wartime Resistance, with Paul Schofield, Marjorie Fielding, Pamela Brown, Michael Goodliffe and Virginia McKenna.

528. *The Innocents*, His Majesty's, 1952. Flora Robson in William Archbold's adaptation of a Henry James story.

529. *A Day By the Sea*, Haymarket, 1953. John Gielgud's production of N. C. Hunter's play, in settings by Felix Kelly.

530. *The Prisoner*, Globe, 1954. Alec Guinness and Noel Willman in Bridget Boland's persecution play.

531. *Man and Superman*, New, 1951. Kay Hammond and John Clements in a revival of Shaw's play.

532. *Separate Tables*, St. James's, 1954. Margaret Leighton and Eric Portman in Terence Rattigan's play.

533. *The Chalk Garden*, Haymarket, 1956. Peggy Ashcroft and Edith Evans in Enid Bagnold's play.

534. *A View From the Bridge*, Comedy, 1956. Anthony Quayle, Mary Ure, Megs Jenkins and Brian Bedford in Arthur Miller's play.

535. *Living Room*, Wyndham's, 1953. Graham Greene's play of religious conflict, with John Robinson, Dorothy Tutin, Eric Portman, Mary Jerrold and Violet Farebrother.

536. *Waiting for Godot*, Arts, 1955. Samuel Beckett's controversial play, with Peter Bull, Timothy Bateson, Paul Daneman and Peter Woodthorpe.

537. *Romanoff and Juliet*, Piccadilly, 1956. Peter Ustinov's political fantasy in a setting by Jean Denis Malclés.

538. *The Mousetrap*, Ambassadors, 1952. Agatha Christie's thriller broke the record run held by *Blithe Spirit* in September 1957.

Index

ACTORS, PLAYWRIGHTS and MANAGERS (The numbers refer to *Picture Captions only*)

Acknowledgments

We would like to thank Mr. Richard Southern for his assistance with pictures and data on theatre buildings, and his unfailing help on many obscure points in the early parts of our text. Our grateful thanks are also due to Mr. George Nash and his staff at the Enthoven Collection, Victoria and Albert Museum; Miss Muriel St. Clair Byrne, for the loan of her photograph of the Macklin Engraving (No. 106); Mrs. Parrish of the *Picture Post Library*; Miss Frances Stephens, for the use of the files of *Theatre World*; Mr. Emile Littler for his good offices in obtaining for us the permission of the Directors of Drury Lane to reproduce the original Charter; Miss Miriam Maisel; Miss Phyllis Mathews, Sir Barry Jackson and Mr. John Trewin, for many kindnesses; and the Art Galleries and owners of original paintings and watercolours, for allowing us to reproduce their possessions. (These are credited under each picture.)

As usual we have to thank Miss Frances Fleetwood for so triumphantly coping with our voluminous manuscript and reducing it to a legible typescript, and for compiling the Index. Our dates, some of which may differ from the usual sources, are mainly drawn from the works of Charles Beecher Hogan, Allardyce Nicoll and the Harvard Catalogue of Dramatic Portraits.

Except for the undermentioned Collections, and the Art Galleries and private owners already noted, the remaining pictures are from our own Collection.

British Museum, Print Room: 39, 50, 60, 88, 121, 177
Enthoven Collection, Victoria & Albert Museum: 67, 93, 95, 98, 110, 123, 125, 143, 146, 159, 186, 192, 201, 271, 272, 274, 275, 276, 279, 371, 376

London Museum, 69
Picture Post Library: 13, 14, 24, 33, 62, 63, 64, 80, 107, 134, 232, 395, 508, 517
Public Record Office: 34
Richard Southern Collection: 2, 4, 9, 10, 11, 12, 37, 92, 119, 120, 124, 129, 153, 170, 231, 248

We wish to thank the following photographers for allowing us to reproduce their work:

Anthony (A. & C. Black): 504, 510
Associated Newspapers, Ltd.: 470
Anthony Buckley: 524
Daniels (by kind permission of the Memorial Theatre, Stratford-upon-Avon): 476
J. W. Debenham: 472, 473, 479, 483, 503
Denis de Marney: 537
Armstrong Jones: 532, 534
Angus McBean: 340, 477, 478, 491, 492, 493, 494, 496, 497, 502, 509, 525, 527, 528, 529, 530, 533, 535, 538
Bertram Park: 456, 484, 485
Houston Rogers: 498, 521, 526, 531, 536
Lenare: 459
Sasha (Cyril Holness): 448, 450, 451, 482, 486
The Times: 6, 458, 495, 518
John Vickers: 505, 506, 507, 513, 514, 515, 519, 520, 522, 523

$20.-